The West Sussex Village Book

THE VILLAGES OF BRITAIN SERIES

Other counties in this series include:

Bedfordshire*
Berkshire*
Buckinghamshire*
Cheshire*
Cleveland*
Cornwall*
Cumbria*
Derbyshire*
Devon*
Dorset
Durham*
Essex*
Glamorgan*
Gloucestershire*
Gwent*
Hampshire*
Herefordshire*
Hertfordshire*
Kent
Lancashire*
Leicestershire
& Rutland*

Lincolnshire*
Norfolk*
Northamptonshire*
Northumberland*
Nottinghamshire*
Oxfordshire*
Powys Montgomeryshire*
Shropshire*
Somerset*
Staffordshire*
Suffolk*
Surrey
East Sussex
Warwickshire*
West Midlands*
Wiltshire*
Worcestershire*
East Yorkshire*
North Yorkshire*
South & West
   Yorkshire*

*Published in conjunction with County Federations of
Women's Institutes

The West Sussex Village Book

TONY WALES

with illustrations by David Thelwell

COUNTRYSIDE BOOKS

NEWBURY, BERKSHIRE

Countryside Books
3 Catherine Road, Newbury, Berkshire.

ISBN 0 905392 34 5

Designed by Mon Mohan

Cover Photograph of South Harting by Ron Oulds
(Spectrum Colour Library)

Produced through MRM Associates Ltd. Reading, Berks.

Printed in Great Britain by
J. W. Arrowsmith Ltd., Bristol.

Acknowledgements

I am grateful to the many people who have helped me with information or by sharing their memories, either in conversation or by correspondence. I am also grateful to the authors of Sussex books and newspaper reports, which I have perused for background knowledge and specific information. At the same time I must particularly thank all those un-named members of Women's Institutes and village societies for the many interesting items of information which they have given me, usually at the end of my talks.

I specifically thank the following for their help. Some are no longer with us, but their names in this list will add a tiny addition to their memorials.

Mr. G. Attrill. Mr. G. Belton. Mr. P. Bench. Mr. R. Blake. Miss M. Boxall. Mrs. W. Cousins. Mr. B. Covey. Mr. C.W. Cramp. Mrs. M. Fyfield. Mr. H. Goatcher. Mr. S. Godman. Mr. & Mrs. Glaysher. Mr. & Mrs. R. Greening. Mr. R.A. Holder. Rev. A. Keith. Mr. T.J. Laker. Mr. S. McCarthy. Mrs. E. Manvell. Mr. T. Mills. Mr. H Mousdell. Mr. & Mrs. P. Nightingale. Mr. R. Ray. Miss I. Shettle. Mrs. I.L. Strudwick. Mrs. J. Sunderland. Mrs. Vincent. Miss F. Woods.

Thanks are also due to the staffs of the Horsham and Crawley Public Libraries, Horsham Museum, The Museum of English Rural Life, Reading and The Sussex Archaeological Society.

Writing even a small book such as this, does tend to take over one's life for a period of time. I am therefore grateful to my family for their understanding, to Nicholas Battle for his encouragement, and of course to David Thelwell for his marvellous illustrations.

If I have inadvertently omitted anyone who should have been included, I sincerely apologise.

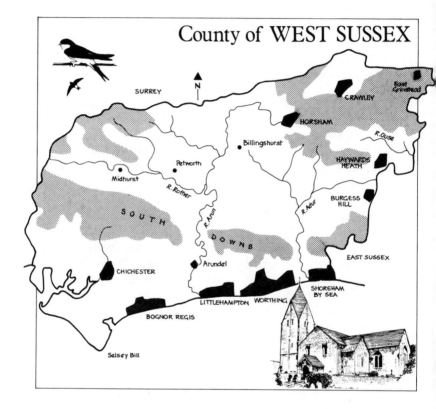

County of WEST SUSSEX

SURREY

N

East Grinstead

C.RAWLEY

HORSHAM

Billingshurst

R. Ouse

HAYWARDS HEATH

Petworth

Midhurst

R. Rother

BURGESS HILL

R. Arun

R. Adur

SOUTH

DOWNS

EAST SUSSEX

CHICHESTER

Arundel

SHOREHAM BY SEA

LITTLEHAMPTON

WORTHING

BOGNOR REGIS

Selsey Bill

Author's Note

'Not another book on Sussex villages?' I can hear you say as you spy this book on a bookseller's shelf. I would be the first to agree that there are rather a lot of Sussex guide books, perhaps even too many. But this particular book is designed to reach the parts that most other guide books do not reach. It will not give you details on architecture, natural history or the best route to follow to reach a particular place. Instead I have concentrated on the traditions, folklore and byways of social history of the villages of West Sussex. Here are the folk stories, the ghosts, the witches, and the bygone beliefs and superstitions connected with specific villages. In addition you will find many of the people who lived in these villages, both famous and infamous. As well as diarists and literary figures, I have included the smugglers – plenty of these – the poachers, the highwaymen and the eccentrics. Undoubtedly I have left a lot out, and even got it all wrong in some cases. But this is inevitable when dealing with the border country of legend and fable, and without living for a lifetime in each village. If so, I apologise, and eagerly await any additions or corrections that readers care to send me.

Some places are included as villages which might be considered towns. No slight is intended. The reason is probably because my own youthful memories are of certain places which were undoubtedly villages then, although they may have moved on to town status since.

In this revised edition of this book I have taken the opportunity to correct a number of minor errors which crept into the original text.

With the help of two readers, I have been able to include some additional information on two of the villages; in the case of Billingshurst I am deeply indebted to Mr J. Dendy Evershed for the valuable material he made available to me. I am also very grateful to Mr Ian Stenning for family recollections concerning the Staplefield shepherds.

I would particularly like to thank all those people who as well as buying and reading the book, took the trouble to write to me to comment on individual items.

Tony Wales
Horsham 1986

Adversane 🌿

I suppose most people would consider life in little Adversane, near Billingshurst, pretty dull in the nineteenth century. But at the annual fair held each September 12th, things were anything but dull. The fair had an annual charter and to make certain that it continued one man put up a single stall each year during the Second World War. In spite of his efforts, the fair finally disappeared in the 1950s.

In its heyday it had horses, pigs, cattle, wheat and corn. Pork was roasted on an open fire, and it was said that no-one thought of eating roast pork before Adversane fair. The roasting mechanism had iron wheels at the top and bottom with a chain passing over them, and a handle to keep it turning.

The fair seems to have been 'all things to all men' with as well as the livestock, crafts and food of all kinds on sale, and of course such things as swingboats, roundabouts, whelk stalls, boxing booths, a wild beast show and many other attractions.

The old Malthouse at Adversane was owned by the Allen Brothers, Alfred and Dennett, who also had premises at Horsham, Worthing, West Chiltington and near Pulborough. They made a fortune by defrauding the government of its rightful excise duty; in fact at all the malthouses owned by the Allens, they did as much business in malt which had not paid duty as they did in excised malt.

Gaius Carley was a well known figure in the village earlier in this century. He was a very important person, the village blacksmith, known and liked by almost everyone in the area. Before settling in Adversane he had worked at a farm and at a forge in Horsham, and then moved on to Kirdford. His experiences included bird scaring for 6s. a week when he was twelve years old, muck spreading, stone picking, hop pole shaving and all types of blacksmith's work, plus surprisingly enough, writing. The latter came about when he was well on in life and he conceived the idea of writing down his own life story.

To start with there seemed little hope of his manuscript being published, and a copy was deposited in the County Record Office for posterity. Then a group of friends decided this was too valuable a record of old village life to remain hidden to all but a few, and his book *The Memories of Gaius Carley, a*

Sussex Blacksmith, written by himself appeared in 1963. It was edited, with a very gentle hand, by Francis Steer and carried a foreword by the Earl of Cottenham. Now the book is a collector's item, much sought after in secondhand bookshops by those who care for old Sussex, and who missed buying it when first published. The book includes a poem by the author *The Song of the Blacksmith,* which begins:

> 'Nearly Sixty Years work in the jolly old forge,
> Sometimes pleasant, sometimes rough,
> Trying to please horses and horsemen,
> It's made me jolly well tough.'

There are eleven more verses in very similar vein. Not very good poetry, but utterly delightful none the less.

Albourne

E.V. Lucas described this village as 'compact, virginal and exquisitely old fashioned'. He also said that it was 'so hidden away, that one might know this part of the country well and yet be continually overlooking it'. In spite of this, or perhaps because of it, one little girl when asked by a school inspector to name the chief festivals of the church, replied 'Christmas, Easter and Albourne Club Day'. Sadly such blissful parochialism has little chance of existing in our country villages today.

Albourne Place is a 17th century brick mansion which Nairn and Pevsner describe as 'curious rather than beautiful'. Bishop Juxon was supposed to have lived here during the Civil War, and on one occasion escaped the Parliamentary troopers by disguising himself as a bricklayer. There is a priests' hole in the chimney, reached by steps in the side of the flue.

Strete Place near Albourne also has a legend of a hiding place in the open fireplace of the great hall. The story is that a horseman being pursued by Parliamentary soldiers, galloped into the hall and almost immediately disappeared from view – complete with horse.

As in many Sussex villages, Albourne once had its own

witch. Her name was Dame Prettylegs, and she was much addicted to placing spells on horses. The fact that her husband was known as a smuggler may have had something to do with the reputation which she cultivated.

A famous inventor was born in Albourne in 1831. He was James Starley, the son of a farmer, who started work on his father's land at the age of nine. When he was fifteen he walked to London, obtaining employment as a gardener. Whilst in this job his inventive bent showed itself, and he went on to work with sewing machines. In 1857, having moved to Coventry, he turned his attention to cycles and tricycles, inventing many new models and improving upon many older ones. He was the great pioneer of the modern cycle and cyclists owe a lot to him. He died in 1881 in Coventry, the city he had made his own.

Aldingbourne ✤

As in so many Sussex villages, the building of greatest interest is the church. St. Mary's is said to be on the site of a 7th century monastery which was built soon after St. Wilfrid's conversion of the South Saxons, and so the village can claim to be one of the oldest centres of Christianity in Sussex.

Ian Nairn and Nikolaus Pevsner in *The Buildings of England – Sussex* (1965) are bitter about the restoration of 1867, calling it 'horrible' and commenting that the windows were 'stamped into the walls with real hatred'. But inside things are better. They mention a carved chair in the chancel, which they think might have come from the colonies as it is so 'outlandish'.

Among the many good stories in *Sussex Church Music in the Past'* by K.H. MacDermott (1922) there are two about Aldingbourne church. The first concerns the time when the two parishes of Aldingbourne and Oving were held jointly by one incumbent, who took the morning service in one church and the afternoon in the other alternately, and it was customary to have no preaching in the morning. A newly appointed vicar decided to introduce a sermon at matins and he informed the choir accordingly. But the sturdy Aldingbourne singers would have 'none of his new-fangled goings-on'. Knowing that there was not much time to spare for the vicar to have his lunch and make the journey to Oving for the afternoon service, they started to sing the 119th psalm as soon as he went into the pulpit to preach. In vain the vicar looked up at the gallery, held up his notes, coughed and hum'd and ha'd. Verse after verse they bawled out lustily, until the vicar's patience and time were exhausted, and he had to climb down, literally and metaphorically. Never was the old Sussex motto 'we wunt be druv' better illustrated.

Aldingbourne is on the edge of what was the Battle of Britain aerodrome of Tangmere, but once it must have been as remote and self sufficient as any other Sussex village. At the beginning of this century the population was about 800, and some idea of the manner in which this little community looked after their own needs is shown by the following list of traders within the village at that time: 7 farmers, 3 cow-keepers, 2 dairymen, 1 farm bailiff, 1 miller, 1 baker (who was also the postman). 3 carpenters or wheelwrights, 2 grocers (both of whom were also drapers), 1 butcher, 2 poulterers, 1 bricklayer, 1 blacksmith, 1 marine store dealer, 1 gardener, 2 harness makers (one also took in lodgers), 1 wood merchant, 2 nurserymen or market gardeners, 1 inn keeper, 2 beer sellers, and at the end of all these very down-to-earth tradesmen, surprisingly − 1 artist.

Aldwick 🌿

Still retaining a little of its own 'villagey' character, although close to Bognor Regis, it includes several old cottages, a nice inn − The Ship and the aptly named Dark Lane, ideal for playing at African safaris, or so it seemed to me as a boy when staying with my aunt at Aldwick. But many of Aldwick's residents live in the new estates, built before and since the Second World War, including what has been dubbed 'The Sussex Riviera' − the Aldwick Bay Estate. This was developed by Captain Allaway in 1928 on what had formerly been rich agricultural land. It was said of one farmer, Henry Upton, that on his land 'not a weed did grow'. Captain Allaway was determined to create 'an outstanding example of land development' and a brochure at the time stated '... for the town dweller who desires a nice type of seaside residence and and for the retired wishing to reside in a peaceful neighbourhood not invaded by trippers and charabanc parties ... free from bands, pierrot parties and the noise and hustle only too commonly associated with many seaside resorts in this country'.

Standards of building were high, although the prices of the houses were astonishingly low judged by today's standards. Partial central heating, verandahs, large garages and telephone cables laid underground to the houses as they were built, were standard. It was expected that each house would have accommodation for staff and chauffeur and each garden large enough for a tennis court.

During King George V's convalescence in 1929 at Craigwell House nearby, Queen Mary drove through the estate, stopped to plant a tree, and admired the old tithe barn, then still standing. This was Swingates Barn which in 1932 was turned into a club for the estate residents. In 1954 the barn caught fire, and but for the determination of the residents would have been completely gutted. It survived, but later succumbed to other pressures and in 1972 was sold for development.

Much of the foregoing is in a very informative history of Aldwick Bay Estate by David Allam, published in 1979.

The nearest thing to an Aldwick ghost story appears in Gerard Young's *The Cottage in the Fields* (1945). It concerns the legend attached to the Campbell family, that when a male member of the family is about to die, three ravens appear on the walls of the castle or wherever he happens to be. In 1934 Sir Duncan Campbell who lived in Aldwick, was ill, and a neighbour saw on the roof of his house 'three miserable looking, drenched ravens'. Shortly afterwards Sir Duncan passed away.

Amberley 🌿

In writing about the Sussex village of Amberley, one is faced with an embarrassment of riches. It has been called a 'show village', 'the pearl of Sussex', 'the loveliest village in Sussex' and 'the artist's village'. The buildings provide an anthology of architecture, with not only an interesting church but a castle next door. Writers have written about it, painters painted it, artists sketched it. In spite of all this, some rustic rhymester was

13

unimpressed except by the quality of its most humble vegetable:

> 'Amberley – God knows,
> All among the rooks and crows,
> Where the good potatoes grows.'

In spite of the beauty of the village, one disadvantage of living there all year round was the strong possiblility of floods in the winter, which were said to result in the women being born with webbed feet. (Presumably the men were not expected to brave the water.) Amberley woman were called 'yellow bellies' by people from other villages, due to their rumoured habit of lifting their skirts to warm themselves over smoky fires. It seems that if you live in a lovely place, then you have to put up with envious neighbours!

Many artists visit Amberley today, just as they have done through the years. The most famous in the past was Edward Stott, born in Rochdale in 1859, who settled in Amberley in 1885, and stayed there until his death in 1918. He was a great walker through the Sussex lanes, often covering eight miles in a day. He seems to have been a typically temperamental artist, with a liking for old clothes until they became nearly ragged, and at one time becoming somewhat of a health food fanatic. But he was a great lover of nature; he guarded the beauties of Amberley most jealously, and he left his wonderful work as a fitting memorial.

No doubt they wassailed their apple trees in Amberley, as in other Sussex villages, but a rhyme collected there in the 1900s proves that the bees were also wassailed. It begins:

> 'Bees, Oh Bees of paradise,
> Does the work of Jesus Christ,
> Does the work which no man can.'

It ends with an injunction to blow the horn, which evidently refers to the practice of blowing cows-horns in wassailing ceremonies.

The church of St. Michael is just outside the castle walls, with its tower overlooking the castle courtyard. The excellent story of Old John Pennicott, bandmaster at the church, has been printed several times, but is worth repeating. On one occasion Pennicott and his bandsmen fell out with the vicar, and although they attended church, they refused to play. From the pulpit the vicar demanded 'Are you going to play or not?' Pennicott answered 'No,' to which the vicar rejoined 'Well then, I'm not going to preach' and came down from the pulpit.

The dispute seems to have gone rather deeply, as after the service was over, the vicar walked down the village street and the bandsmen followed with their instuments and gave him 'rough music.' On another occasion the band went on strike completely and refused to attend or play in church. The vicar called on all publicans and persuaded them to refuse to serve any of the bandsmen. They in turn retaliated by white-washing the vicar's windows all over during the night. I have a copy of a picture of John Pennicott playing his clarionet, and he has the look of a man determined enough to have acted in the way these stories suggest.

Amberley – Belgian Kilns & Dobbin cart
Amberley Chalk Pits

Amberley with its old buildings must have several ghost stories, but one concerns the vicarage which was said to be haunted by the ghost of a young girl. During the First World War, bones of a young girl and an old man were discovered under the floor boards. Legend says that in the 18th century the bishop ordered the vicar of the time to end a liaison with a young woman.

The castle is an impressive building, although less 'fairy-tale like' than Arundel. It was a palace of the Bishops of Chichester throughout the Middle Ages, before Bishop Rede decided to 'crenellate' or fortify it in 1377. Whether he feared attacks from pirates sailing up the Arun, or just fancied a castle-like dwelling we do not know, but he made a good job of it, and it is now scheduled as an ancient monument.

Visitors to the village today have yet one more attraction. This is the Chalk Pits Museum of the Southern Industrial History Centre Trust, which is close to the railway station on the main road, on the site of the old lime-burning quarries. The museum aims to include representative working exhibits of all types of historical industry in Sussex, and every year since its inception more and more fascinating things have been added. A history of lime burning and the Amberley Chalk Pits Museum was published by the West Sussex County Council in 1979.

The Arun is close at hand, and fishing and boating have attracted visitors for a long time. One of Fuller's 'seven good things of Sussex' was an Amberley trout.

The village has been well documented. In 1923 by the Rev. H. Rickard in *Amberley: its castle, church and history,* and in 1968 by the Rev. E. Noel Staines in his delightfully named *Dear Amberley,* and about the same period by Wilfred E. Cheal in *Amberley Heritage.*

Angmering ᘯ

Angmering is a neat village, with the archetypal village green, and many lovely old houses and cottages clustering round it.

The church of St. Margaret is said to have been restored by the local squire with the proceeds of a Derby win. It once had a musical vicar, the Rev. William Kinleside, who was the incumbent from 1776 to 1836. He played the cello, and often drove to Chichester to attend concerts. In view of the state of Sussex roads at the time, even a journey of this length must have been a serious undertaking.

Angmering has the almost obligatory tunnel legend. The passage is supposed to lead in two directions, to a house in Church Row and to the rear of Church House in Arundel Road.

In the 1920s and 1930s, the traditional Sussex May Day customs were largely superseded by celebrations on Empire Day (May 24th). At Angmering, the school children danced from the village hall up the hill to a field, where they danced round a maypole. The girls had head-dresses and frocks with real flowers on them.

The public house, the Spotted Cow, has a long history, and was reputed to be the haunt of smugglers. The pub has a spinning jenny on one of the ceilings, and one of the conjectured uses of this was the division by smugglers of their spoils. Other suggestions include a game, or to decide who should pay for a round of drinks.

West Sussex as seen through the eyes of the W.I. (1973) includes a vast amount of local social history, culled from members' memories. One story therein concerning Angmering, is of a resident's great great grandmother, who sat demurely sewing in her crinoline whilst underneath was a bolt of French silk forty yards in length. Tea was also smuggled into the village, hidden in blue Bristol glass rolling pins, secreted down innocent looking trouser legs.

Chants Cottage in the High Street serves as a reminder of Mr. Chant, a well known local shepherd who lived there and brought up ten children. One of their meals was provided by docked lambs' tails, which would have been stripped and boiled to make a jelly.

Ardingly 🐝

Three lies and all true? Ardingly, Chiddingly and Hoathly (of course you can substitute other places ending in 'ly' if you choose.) This old riddle only works because Sussex folk always pronounced 'ly' as 'lie' and not 'lee'. The addition of 'sure-lie'

17

with the accent on the second syllable, at the end of a sentence, was the old Sussex equivalent of the ubiquitous 'you know' of the present day.

Many may think first of Wakehurst Place when Ardingly is mentioned. The older parts of the house date from 1590 and were built by Sir Edward Culpeper – of the same family as Nicholas of the famous *Herbal*. The house and gardens are now in the care of the National Trust, and the latter of 170 acres are visited by thousands of garden lovers every year. The sandstone outcrop which runs along the south brow of the valley, has provided huge blocks of stone overhanging a steep bank. The yew trees make this dark, cool and mysterious.

Ardingly College, one of the three Woodard schools in the county, was opened in 1870. The buildings are of red brick in the shape of two courtyards. The chapel which was completed in 1883 is notable, although not as great as Lancing.

Thomas Box, a famous cricketer, was born at Ardingly, and the author George Forrester Scott (who wrote as John Hailsham) lived here. He wrote *Lonewood Corner* and *Idehurst*. The former was set in Ardingly, and the latter in Lindfield. *Idehurst* is subtitled *a journal kept in the country* and is just that; an unpretentious account of old country life (it was published in 1898), full of wisdom and altogether delightful, although even then wistful for the 'good old days'.

Ashington ✍

A small village straddling the main Horsham to Worthing road, and with some buildings including the church of St. Peter and St. Paul, lying to the west.

Living in a cottage on the main road is a friend of mine known to many as 'old Harry', although he is no more than middle-aged. Harry came originally from Lancashire, but has so assimilated Sussex and Sussex ways that one is apt to forget his 'foreign' origins. He was a founder member of what was probably the first folk song club in Sussex at the start of the modern folk song revival, and Father Christmas in its Mummers play. He was very much involved both in organising and as chairman of the Horsham Folk Festivals which were held for several consecutive years. He became an enthusiastic member of the Chanctonbury Ring Morris Men, and was in at the beginning of the Broadwood Morris Men, serving as Squire and Bagman in subsequent years. 'Old Harry' has made his name well known in many Sussex villages as a barn dance caller – a role which many years ago he confided in me he would never be able to fill, as he had too bad a memory to remember the dances! Now with his tambourine and his 'jig doll' he is welcome whenever a group or club are lucky enough to be able to book him up on one of his rare 'free' weekends. The 'jig doll' was a happy inspiration to fill a break in the dancing, and is based on a traditional 'little dancing man'. It has freely movable arms and legs and is held by a dowel which slots into its back. It dances easily to jigs (or reels) and is set in motion by one of Harry's hands moving up and down on a thin pliable piece of wood on which the doll is supported.

The cottage where Harry lives in Ashington was once the home of another local 'character', Cyril Morley, who had a small-holding on ground now taken up by houses, and named appropriately Morley Close.

Ashurst ༄

A secluded village in an area essentially agricultural in character with plenty to please lovers of trees and woods. A list of 1903, devoted to commercial activities in the village, showed that the majority of residents were involved in farming work of one kind or another.

The church of St. James on a by-road, is unique in Sussex in still having a vamp-horn (there are only five others in the rest of England). The instrument, if it can be so described, is a single tube made of tin, 3 feet in length and 7 inches across the bell. Painted green, it bears the inscription 'Praise him upon ye strings and pipe, 1770, Palmer Fecit'. Opinions vary as to the exact use to which these curious horns were put. Probably they were used for amplifying the singing, rather like a megaphone. Other suggestions include to call the cattle home from the church tower, to call people to church, to summon assistance in time of danger or to reinforce the sound of the band or choir in the church. The particular shape of the Ashurst vamp-horn is unusual, compared with the other examples from the rest of the country.

Margaret Fairless Barber, who wrote the famous Sussex book *The Roadmender* under the name of Michael Fairless, is buried in Ashurst churchyard.

Balcombe 🦋

Although on the main London – Brighton rail line, Balcombe still retains much of its village character. The country is well wooded, with sparkling streams, hammer ponds and lakes. Within the area are several chalybeate springs, once renowned for their medicinal qualities, including one which was supposed to equal in quality the better known springs at Tunbridge Wells. Stone was once extensively quarried in the neighbourhood.

Many villages have treasure legends, but Balcombe has a true story from 1897 of a metal pot containing 12 gold and over 700 silver coins, being found in the village, and claimed by the crown as treasure-trove.

The local ghost story is of a labourer who hanged himself from a tree in a meadow, and who appears thus to unsuspecting villagers from time to time. The branch on which the unfortunate man hung himself was later struck by lightning, but continues to appear whole in each ghostly apparition.

The coming of the railway to this lovely countryside must have been resisted by many, but nowadays the 1,475 feet long viaduct across the valley of the river Ouse – now narrow, but once wide enough to carry barges – is considered a thing of beauty and a very important piece of historic railway architecture. Built in 1839-41, it has 37 brick arches, which although they now carry much greater weights and volume than was originally anticipated, are still as staunch and firm as when they were built.

A railway journey in this part of Sussex is not without variety; in addition to the handsome viaduct there is the 1,333 yards of Balcombe railway tunnel. As a young boy I was worried by the thought of being stuck in the tunnel, a possibility not impossible according to my aunt who related tales of such happenings in the past. In fact one such incident was reported in the *Sussex County Magazine* in 1940, when a contributor described how in the days when the well-to-do folk often travelled in their own private coaches atop a railway truck added to the end of the train, a certain man found his truck uncoupled in Balcombe tunnel. All his shouting was in vain, but after what seemed an eternity he saw to his horror an engine with whistle screaming, steaming towards him. He almost collapsed with relief when he found that it was a pilot engine sent to rescue him.

The building of these tunnels and viaducts must have been a vast undertaking, with hordes of 'navvies' (originally 'canal navigators' and now building the upstart railway), descending on a quiet country area and for a time completely disrupting its peaceful existence. Casualties must have been almost commonplace, such as that reported by a Sussex paper, when William Hanbury, a navvy working on the London, Brighton and South Coast Railway, was killed by a portion of the bank which was being excavated, falling on him. The inquest was held at the Half Moon Inn, Balcombe on June 17th 1839.

A old local saying is that 'it is sure to rain when the rector cuts his front field.' One of the rectors, the Rev. Douglas L. Secretan wrote a short but interesting history of his church and rectory in 1937. The rector obviously had a good sense of humour, as he began by recounting an old Sussex belief that when a clergyman is inducted to a living he will reign over the parish for as many years as he tolls the church bell. He goes on to say that he came to Balcombe in 1909 and solemnly tolled the bell according to custom, afterwards being informed that he had rung it but 13 times. At the time of writing he had been rector for 25 years, but he felt that his real term of office was over after the first 13 years, and that ever since then the parish had really been ruled by the Church Council and similar bodies!

Barnes Green

A small village ignored by most books on Sussex, with a predictably large village green and a useful hall, which houses among other events an annual art exhibition which attracts support from a wide area.

The village clubs were the forerunners of one aspect of today's welfare state. Men paid in a few pence weekly, usually at the 'local' and drew benefit when they were prevented from working by illness. No dole or social security then, of course. The highspot of the village year was often the annual Club Day, when the members met for a parade followed by a feast at the pub. Sometimes so large a part of the club funds were swallowed up by the meal that there was little left to pay out benefit.

I am sure this never happened at Barnes Green, where the club day was held on the third Monday in July and was described to me as 'the biggest day in the year'. It was a school holiday, and the members paraded wearing rosettes, led by a man in a white smock and a local band. There were many stops for liquid refreshment, until finally the church at Itchingfield was reached for a special service. This was followed by mince pies and coffee at the Rectory and then on to Muntham for lunch in a big marquee. The night before had been given over to a 'Cherry Fair' in the pub, and on the day of the procession there was an open-air fair on the green. One jarring note in an otherwise happy day was the annoyance caused by members who used the churchyard for unconventional purposes – but rather necessary after all that beer, as there were no public toilets in those days.

All this came to an end just before the Second World War, and the club was finally wound up in 1977 after an existence of 126 years; a casualty of the welfare state. The amount of cash to be shared out in 1977 was the surprisingly large sum of £6,000, which was carefully divided between the 36 remaining members.

Barnham 🦚

Many people know this village merely as a junction on the main line from Victoria to the coast; in fact one of the happy memories of my own childhod was hearing a porter calling out at, I think, Arundel, 'Littlehampney, Barney and Bogney' when travelling by rail for a holiday at either Littlehampton or Bognor.

The Barnham tower mill has been a local landmark since it was built in 1829 replacing an earlier post mill. Just before the turn of the century the mill was taken over by John Baker and remained in the ownership of the Baker family for some years. A Sussex Directory of 1903 gives the motive power as wind and steam, but in 1919 all working from wind had ceased, and in 1926 a gas engine was fitted. The sweeps remained in position at that time, but eventually they were taken down. During the 1930s the mill must have been a conspicuous and pretty sight, with the cap painted white against the black of the tower, and other parts picked out in red. In its hey-day 11 other working windmills could be seen from the top of Barnham mill, but when the army used it as a lookout during the last war, there would have been none.

Bersted (North and South)

Twin villages, now with little of their original character, having become virtually suburbs of Bognor Regis. Ironically, South Bersted was the original village of Bognor. In the 1780s Sir Richard Hotham, a rich hatter from Southwark, bought a farm there and started to develop the area. He died and is buried at South Bersted, after spending £60,000 on his schemes, but failing to change the name Bognor to Hothampton.

Some people will think of the Stamp House when they hear mention of North Bersted. This contained a huge collection of stamps of every country, made by Mr. Richard Sharpe, starting in 1882. Unfortunately the stamps were not neatly hinged in albums but were stuck all over the walls, the ceilings and the furniture; even on screens or strung up in the form of serpents.

In some cases the stamps were arranged in the form of designs such as Queen Victoria's portrait or the coat of arms of Bognor. It was evidently intended as a big tourist attraction, and several different designs of picture postcards showing the rooms, the exterior and the gardens of the Stamp House, were on sale. As a child I heard about the place and longed to visit it, but of course by that time it had ceased to exist. But no one seems to know what became of all those stamps.

Bignor 🌿

A small village which features in all the Sussex guide books by reason of its justly famous Roman Villa which was found in 1811 by a young man ploughing in his father's fields, known as The Berry and Town Field. He came upon a tesselated pavement of considerable beauty, and this led to the eventual discovery of one of the finest examples of Roman architecture in this part of England. The village is on the line of Stane Street and Roman remains had long been suspected although nothing or real importance had previously been reported. The villa was completely excavated in the 1920s and was found to cover over 4 acres. In 1740 elephant bones had been dug up at Bignor, so it is considered possible that the Romans used elephants at the villa. The most interesting of the remains are the mosaics, which are of very fine quality.

Another interesting relic of the past at Bignor is the exceedingly well known village shop, a 15th century cottage which later became a grocer's shop; well known because it features on so many calendars and in so many pictorial books on Sussex.

Bignor Park was the home of Nicholas Turner, the father of the now rather neglected novelist and poet, Charlotte Smith. She later lived at Bignor and in several other places in Sussex, so we can claim her as one of our writers.

Bignor Hill has one of the lesser known Sussex dragon legends attached to it. It was said that the dragon or huge serpent used to coil itself round the hill, and that the marks of its coils could be plainly seen. This belief was probably prompted by the marks of sheep tracks around the hill.

Billingshurst 🖋

Some may consider it a small town in view of its modern shopping centre, public library, and car park. But I have one particular memory of Billingshurst in the 1930s, when as a boy on a summer's day I saw the whole High Street and diminutive Green completely covered by sheep as they were being driven through. Undoubtedly it was a village then, and so it remains one in my mind.

There are several fine old houses, some still with Horsham Stone 'slab' roofs. Ye Olde Six Bells is a 16th century half timbered inn, which may have been named after the original 6 bells of the parish church – although the number was increased to 8 in 1892. The church once had its own band, including a bass viol. One old lady who died in 1918 aged 82 remembered how as a child she always imagined that God himself lived inside the big fiddle.

Another old story concerning the church tells of how each Sunday certain parishioners 'raced' each other for favourite seats in the chancel. The schoolmaster did not have to take part in these unseemly proceedings, as he had his own carved chair in one of the galleries.

The Unitarian church in the High Street is one of the oldest chapels in the south of England. It was built in 1754, and in 1880 an open-air baptistry was made into a library where children came to lessons, as there was no village school. The long table used then is still to be seen, as is also the chapel clock made by Inkpen of Horsham in 1756. Memories of school in Billingshurst early in this century include a picture of the lady teacher who was not much over 4 feet tall. Some of her pupils were 6 foot youths and when they misbehaved she would chase them round the blackboard which was on a central swivel. The boys would duck underneath, and swing the board as they did so, in order to crack the teacher on the head as she tried to follow them. When she eventually caught them, they would receive a well-deserved beating, in spite of her tiny stature. When they got home, and if they were unwise enough to admit to having been beaten at school, they would most likely get another from their father.

Like so many Sussex towns and villages, Billingshurst has

always enjoyed November 5th. One of its two windmills, at the back of the Six Bells, was burnt down on November 5th 1852. Although whether this had anything to do with the date we can only conjecture. One particular custom at Billingshurst was for a man dressed as a devil to run to the top of the bonfire as the villagers recited their Bonfire Hymn – and then run down as fast as possible before he got caught in the flames. The tradition came to an end one year when the 'devil' was badly burned.

Another old custom was carried out on Shrove Tuesday, when villagers threw at tethered cocks. Late in the 18th century the Rev. William Evershed, pastor of the Unitarian church, wrote a 26-line poem entitled *The Cock's Remonstrance on Shrove-Tuesday*, and pinned it to the church door. It had the desired effect, and soon afterwards the practice was abandoned.

Perhaps even in a village as attractive as Billingshurst, these were not really the 'good old days'. Man traps were in use until 1867, and in 1863 a labourer's wife wrote to a Sussex paper complaining that her total income was 12s for a week, and she had to keep herself, her husband and four children. Rent was 2s. 6d. a week, at least 1s on fuel and 3d for soap and soda, leaving 8s. 3d. for food, shoes and clothing.

Birdham

An inconspicuous place until the 1930s when the fashion for leisure sailing brought prosperity to this and other similar villages in the Chichester Harbour area. Until quite recent times it had the last working tidal mill in Sussex, but this has been taken over by the yachtsmen.

The much restored church of St. James has a door in the north wall, known as a 'Devil's Door' due to the old belief that if it was left open at christenings the Devil, who had been hoping to possess the unbaptised child's soul, would depart in haste.

Canon MacDermott in *Sussex Church Music in the Past* (1922) tells a favourite story. A violinist in Birdham church band, a hot-headed old gentleman, put a lot of enthusiasm into his playing. On one occasion during a service, a string broke and in his exasperation he flung his instrument from the choir gallery into the nave of the church, shouting 'Goo down there and bide there,' and he refused to play any more.

Bolney 🌿

Bolney is not very big, but what there is pleases the eye. The once infamous Bolney crossroads are no more – the busy Brighton road now crosses the east-west road by means of a bridge, a change which was greeted by a universal sigh of relief from both Bolney residents and passing motorists. The main street has the 13th century church of St. Mary Magdalene with a sturdy lychgate made of Sussex oak, Sussex marble, Sussex millstones and Horsham stone. The village is famous for its bells and bellringers; the church has 8 bells (as has the village pub sign) and E. V. Lucas in his *Highways and Byways of Sussex* (1904) provides the following satisfying quote: 'Those who are fond of the silvery tones of bells, may enjoy them to perfection, by placing themselves on the margin of a large pond, the property of Mr. W. Marshall; the reverberation of the sound, coming off the water, is peculiarly striking.'

A famous collector of rare books, Henry Huth, whose collection fetched £300,000 when it was sold in 1910, once lived at Wykehurst Place; surely one of the most unlikely houses to be found anywhere in Sussex. It was built in 1872 at a cost of £35,000 in the style of a French chateau. The effect from a short distance is absolutely fairytale; something out of the classic folk tales of Europe; a veritable castle of a house – but completely unlike any of the other castles in our county. In spite of its relatively small cost by present day standards, it is doubtful if anyone could afford to build anything like it today. Naturally film-makers love it, and it has been featured in several productions. My first view of Wykehurst was when it was still derelict and damaged after being used by troops during the 1939-45 war, but even in this less than perfect state, it was still a very exciting sight.

Bosham 🌿

Bosham must be one of the most historically important villages in Sussex, or so the many legends associated with it would have us believe.

The Venerable Bede records that even before St. Wilfrid

brought Christianity to Sussex, a monk by the name of Dicul had a small monastery at or near Bosham. It is also the place where Sussex legend insists King Canute ordered the waves to retreat from his royal feet, although several other counties disagree.

Canute was supposed to have lived in Bosham, and it seems likely that his daughter was buried in the church. The story of the discovery of her coffin has been told many times, but is well worth re-telling. It had long been believed by old Bosham residents that the 8 year old princess was interred within the church, and during the restoration of the building, the Rev. Henry Mitchell took the opportunity to investigate the site which some of his parishioners insisted was the place of her burial. The floor was taken up on August 4th 1865, and a stone coffin was found. The lid was removed, unfortunately breaking in two, and the remains of a child of about the right age were found. The coffin corresponded in style with coffins of Canute's period. It was on show to visitors for several weeks, and was then closed and reinterred.

In 1954 the coffin was again investigated, but upon it being opened no bones were found, and it was assumed that the earlier opening had caused them to disintegrate, although it was even suggested that this was not the same coffin. Only a glass bottle containing a small quantity of brown liquid was found within the coffin, and this has remained something of a mystery, as it had not been mentioned in accounts of the 1865 investigation. At the same time a larger coffin made of Horsham stone was discovered 3 feet away from the smaller one. It contained bones from a powerfully built man aged about 60, with traces of arthritis. Another local tradition had long stated that Earl Godwin, King Harold's father was buried here, and he is known to have walked with a limp.

Yet another of the fascinating Bosham stories is that it was from Quay Meadow that Harold embarked for Normandy in 1064. Substance is added to this story by the fact that Harold and Bosham church are shown on the Bayeux tapestry.

Still another legend concerns the Bosham church bells. In the days of the Northmen, a band of pirates came pillaging up the creek. They seized one of the bells from the church, and made off with it in their ship in spite of the entreaties of the villagers. The remaining bells were rung either in thanksgiving for the deliverance of the people, or as a curse on the vandals. Immediately the stolen bell broke loose and crashed through the deck of the ship on which it was being carried, and sank beneath the waves in what is now known as 'Bell Hole'. It remains there to this day, and when the existing bells are rung, the sunken one is said to chime in unison. The sequel is that at a later date a wise man (the male version of a white witch) was called upon to help recover the bell. He told the villagers to dredge it up from the deep with ropes pulled by a team of white oxen, who could be relied on for a strong but steady pull. However, one oxen had one black hair, and so the ropes snapped and the bell sank back beneath the waves.

An enormous pole was once suspended horizontally inside the nave of the church, and was supposed to be the staff of Bevis, the legendary Sussex giant, who used to stride across Bosham harbour in one step. When the Rev. K. H. MacDermott wrote his history of Bosham church in 1926, there was still within the memory of the oldest inhabitants the sluggard waker's wand. This was used in the church by the parish clerk to awaken with a gentle tap on the head, those who preferred to sleep during the sermon.

As in other villages the churchyard was at one time the place where adults and children played games, cattle were grazed, fishermen mended their nets, washing was hung out to dry and fights took place. All this ended when a wall was built to enclose the sacred ground.

In spite of Bosham's early connections with Christianity, in 1825 a group of villagers felt compelled to write:

> The village of Bosham was until 1812 proverbial
> for ignorance and wickedness, there being no
> gospel either in the established church or out of it.'

For these reasons they held a Congregational Church service in the village for the first time.

Bosham has a buried treasure legend to the effect that Cavalier money and jewels from the time of the Civil War are buried in the Manor House. This same building also has several ghost stories, including one about an old man who died sitting gazing out of a certain window, waiting for his son to return from sea after they had quarrelled. There were also stories of a secret tunnel linking the Manor House and the vault of the church, although these have apparently never been substantiated.

During the time of the Great Plague of 1664, the inabitants of Chichester closed the city gates to prevent the spread of the disease. The fishermen of Bosham heard of their plight, and left food outside the gates regularly, until the plague subsided. For this they were allowed to sell their fish in the Chichester market without fee. Fishing and Bosham have always been closely associated, and once there was a flourishing oyster industry. Now these have become scarce, although experts do not agree on the reason.

Bosham had its gang of 'tipteerers' or Christmas mummers, up until the late 19th century. There were about 20 of them, who acted, sang and danced each Boxing Day. They wore smocks and 'chummies' (round black felt hats worn by Sussex men), and they started out at about 9.00 in the morning in decorated farm carts for Shopwyke House, where they were entertained all day, until 9.00 in the evening. They were cheered on their way, particularly through Chichester.

Bosham is now a very popular place with the yachting fraternity, and also attracts many other visitors. It is most pleasant at high tide, when the mud flats are hidden, but that can prove unfortunate for some. I have seen cars with the waves lapping their roofs – left in forbidden places in spite of the plentiful warning notices.

Locally Bosham is pronounced 'Bossum', although I once had difficulty in explaining to the R.A.C. on the phone exactly where I had broken down, when I used the correct Sussex pronunciation.

Bosham is altogether delightful. Even Tennyson thought so, when he made Becket say:-

> 'Better to have been a fisherman at Bosham, my good Herbert,
> Thy birthplace – the sea creek – the petty rill,
> That falls into it – the green field – the gray church –
> the simple lobster basket and the mesh.'

Boxgrove 🪻

The Benedictine priory which has now become the parish church of St. Mary and St. Blaise, has been extolled in many books on Sussex. Suffice to say that it is one of the jewels of the county, and should be on every tourist's visiting list.

Canon MacDermott tells us that when the church had its band of 'musicianers', they stood originally around the pulpit. Later they migrated to the choir gallery, and as soon as they began playing the whole congregation turned round 'to face the music'. Surely a sincere compliment to the players, if not exactly respectful to the celebrant.

There are several other buildings of interest in the village; for instance the Almshouses, dating from the 18th century, built by the Countess of Derby who lived at Halnaker House.

Sussex cricket has deep roots in Boxgrove, some people even think it all started here. Certainly it is recorded as having been played by several named players in the churchyard during Evensong on 28th April 1622, and the Sunday following. Quite obviously this did not meet with the approval of the churchwardens, in fact they maintained that it was against the 7th article; there was also the matter of broken windows, and lastly there was the small child who nearly had her brains beaten out with a cricket bat.

Many Sussex villages had their mummers or 'tipteers' play at Christmas time. The name seems to have been peculiar to Sussex, and no one seems to know its real origin, although it has been suggested (not very convincingly I feel) that it comes from the old word for cloak; tippet. Most of the plays disappeared during the 19th century, but some have been revived from time to time. One of the first of what might be termed the modern revivals was at Boxgrove. However, this revival really went back to East Preston, when in 1911 Mr. Foard, a farmhand, remembered how as a boy he had been one of the gang led by an old man named Barnard. The old chap took the part of Father Christmas in the play, and also sent his boys out with a Guy on November 5th. He kept the money collected at both times and the boys had to be content with sweets as a reward. Mr. Foard could remember most of the East Preston play, but there were some gaps in his memory. But with the help of a copy of the

Iping play, a complete version was made up, which the East Preston men used each Christmas for several years.

The Great War came and the East Preston play was again forgotten, until one of the participants, on his return, decided to revive the play yet again, but this time at Boxgrove. He was the fiddler, Mr. R. J. Sharp, and at his instigation the Boxgrove tipteers met once a week to learn the play and sing Sussex songs. On 9th January 1937 they were invited to take their play to a much larger audience at the Silver Jubilee Festival of the English Folk Dance and Song Society, in the Royal Albert Hall, London.

The sight of the Boxgrove men in their costumes and the old words, prompted many recollections from elderly people in their audiences, and to their delight one man commented that the Boxgrove tipteers 'be 'bout the same as they was'.

A Sussex newspaper report of 16th November 1938 mentions the Boxgrove tipteers, who were then in their 12th season of revival, and that they also sang 'The Jolly Woodcutter', 'Littlehampton Collier', and 'Sweet Rosy Morn',

In 1939-45 war again disrupted the Boxgrove mummers' activities, but in more recent times there have been many revivals of the Sussex tipteers plays, inspired in some cases no doubt, by memories of the Boxgrove gang of the 1930s.

Bramber

Bramber is a very attractive place, although it consists almost entirely of just one village street. Until the 1920s flooding in winter was a way of life. Many picture postcards from the early part of this century still turn up, showing views of Bramber covered by flood waters. They show pictures of residents in rowing boats fetching their provisions, or the local policeman making his rounds in a boat. In February 1904 there was a particularly bad flood, but the locals turned the disaster into an enjoyable day out by organising a tub race to Beeding.

Once Bramber was a seaport of some importance on the river Adur. Then its importance and population dropped to a low ebb – it had but 162 inhabitants in 1903 – until it became a popular place of pilgrimage for 20th century tourists.

Bramber in 1905

The romantic looking remains of a Norman castle stand in an attractive setting on a mound overlooking the village street and the church of St. Nicholas, which was damaged in 1642 by Cromwell's men. One of the most important buildings is St. Mary's House, which has been described as one of the finest timber-framed buildings in Sussex. Until very recently it housed the National Butterfly Museum, but this has recently been sold. St. Mary's has a tradition of the future King Charles II spending a night in a certain room, on his flight through Sussex during the Civil War. What is more certain is that he did at least pass through Bramber on his way to the coast.

'Old Clem's Night' on November 23rd was the traditional blacksmith's day in Sussex. One man told me how the local boys at Bramber made an effigy of 'Old Clem', put him in a chair and carried him round the houses begging for apples and beer. In 1926 an old woman from Bramber gave a similar account to the author Arthur Beckett, adding that after carrying the figure round and 'firing the anvil', they took 'Old Clem' to the door of the Public Bar, and left him propped up there while they had their supper. The St. Clements' Day feast was important to Sussex blacksmiths, and celebrations similar to the ones at Bramber were carried out in many Sussex villages. The supper or feast usually ended with the singing by the company of the blacksmith's anthem, the song 'Twankydillo'.

Bramber was once a rotten borough and parliamentary elections were something of a farce. George Spencer, writing about the Bramber election of 1679 said 'You would have laughed to see how pleased I seemed to be in kissing of old women; and drinking wine with handfuls of sugar, and great glasses of burnt brandy'. It was even said that one cottager refused £1000 for his vote. The much respected William Wilberforce was once driving through Bramber and seeing the name, he thought it was vaguely familiar. He then suddenly recollected that it was the place for which he sat in Parliament. A much told story, probably apocryphal, but typical of the times.

Bramber has a wealth of legends, and several of them are told at some length by Herbert T. Erredge in *History and Legends of Bramber Castle*. These rather verbose accounts have been neatly condensed in a more modern work by John G. Garratt *Bramber and Steyning* (1973) which I can thoroughly recommend.

A local ghost story tells of a white horse which Bramber residents claim to have seen galloping round the dried-up moat of the castle on moonlight nights. One man told John Garratt 'we 'ears 'is 'oofs, too'.

There is also the almost obligatory tunnel story related in connection with the castle. A certain old man just before he died recalled how as a boy he had entered the passage from the moat, but became frightened and returned without penetrating to the end.

A more modern story connected with the occult dates from 1964, when the churchyard of St. Nicholas was desecrated by a stone cross weighing nearly a hundredweight being taken from a grave and propped against the church door. Statues of angels had their heads broken off, and signs said to be connected with black magic were chalked on the flagstones of the church porch. The vicar (and who would blame him) solemnly placed a curse on the vandals at the following Sunday's church service. Later he said he would lift the curse as the culprits had cleaned up the mess in the churchyard, and attempted to repair the damage. However, the police claimed responsibility for the clean up, but not until the whole affair had become national news.

A Sussex guide book at the beginning of the century described it as a 'model ornithological museum', but it is remembered more as a charming but distinctly odd curiosity. I am speaking of course of Bramber's most famous tourist attraction, Potter's Museum, which was begun by Mr. Walter Potter, a self taught taxidermist, in 1861. The first museum consisted of 98 species of British birds, and was in a summerhouse behind the inn, kept by his father. In 1866 it was moved into a purpose-built building, and it remained there until 1880 when it was again moved, this time to a larger home. The exhibition grew all the time, and consisted very largely of tableaux of stuffed baby animals in human situations. For instance there was the 'Kitten's Tea Party', the 'Lower Five or Rat's Den' and the 'Death and Burial of Cock Robin'. An old guide to the museum lists 239 exhibits, plus many more un-numbered. As well as the stuffed animals, there were all sorts of other curiosities such as leg irons from Lewes prison, a skin of a water hog killed at Steyning mill stream in 1915, a baker's oven lamp found at Bramber in 1780 and much more of the same. This very unusual accumulation was sold in 1970 when the grandson of the founder died. The building at Bramber then housed a museum of a very different kind, although still of tremendous interest. It became the 'House of Pipes' and devoted to exhibits connected with every aspect of smoking. Sad to say, this has also now passed into Bramber's history.

Bramber once appeared in a detective novel *The Music Gallery Murder* by R.J. Forster, where it was thinly disguised as Bramfold.

Broadbridge Heath 🌿

Like most main road villages, Broadbridge Heath suffered from the 20th century curse of heavy traffic on its doorstep, until summer 1983 when a bypass relieved it of all but local traffic and those few motorists who avoid bypass roads on principle. Now everyone in the village must be much happier, except perhaps the owners of the petrol stations on the village road.

Wickhurst Lane was neatly cut into two by the bypass, but the second section still leads to Broadbridge farm with its beautiful little barn, nowadays used by its owner for private social functions and lent to the local police for their annual barn dance. Barns of this kind must have been used for dances and feasts through their history, although during most of their time they would have been taken up with more mundane matters.

In spite of the closeness of Broadbridge Heath to its big neighbour Horsham, it has retained its own identity and once a year many of the separate village activities come together in a big fete on the Green. Back in the last century the Broadbridge Heath Club Feast was one of the best in the area. Many Horsham people came to it, just as they come to the village fete today. The members of the club dressed in white smocks and fluffy beaver pot hats, many of them carrying a peeled willow staff, marched in procession to the Horsham parish church and back again to Broadbridge Heath for their feast and amusements. They all wore a coloured ribbon bow, and must have made a fine sight as they passed up Horsham's Bishopric, then known as the Rookery, to the old church in the Causeway.

The village is fortunate today in having its own fine school, named after the poet Shelley who was born at Field Place close by. I have been privileged to visit the school a few times in recent years, and have been carried away by the strong feeling of happy activity throughout the school. It is very much a part of the local community, and some idea of how this has been achieved over the years can be discovered in the booklet produced by the school in 1983 to mark its centenary. The extracts from the old log books printed in the book, show not only how the school functioned in its early days, but are also a valuable insight into the social history of a Sussex village.

Absences were once very common. In January 1873 several children were absent through going for soup (evidently soup kitchens were necessary that year); in February it was chilblains which kept some away. In July haymaking and attending local galas were blamed, and later in the year it was acorn gathering time. Then there were soldiers passing through on their way to Horsham, the Forester's Fete, lack of boots, gleaning in the fields, swede pulling, May Day flower gathering and of course 'hopping' in Kent. All given as reasons for absence from school, most one supposes with the full knowledge of the parents.

Sometimes there was excitement. In February 1876 a judge came to investigate bribery in a recent election, and then there was the girl who was 'whipped to school' by her mother, screaming and kicking all the way but calming down once she was left at school.

Broadwater 🦋

We may find it hard to believe, but Broadwater was once the nucleus of Worthing; in fact a book of 1835 speaks of Worthing as a hamlet of Broadwater parish.

Sussex folklore is full of stories about running seven times around certain places or things, in order to tempt the devil out. Sometimes certain conditions must be observed, such as running at midnight, on midsummer-eve or backwards. The oldest tomb in Broadwater churchyard shares this doubtful honour, although I have never heard any reason to account for the legend.

Another eerie tale relating to Broadwater has been quoted in several books on Sussex, but I think the original account was in Mrs. Charlotte Latham's *Some West Sussex Superstitions lingering in 1868*. Her own words are worth quoting:

> 'There stood, and still may stand, upon the downs, close to Broadwater, an old oak tree, that I used, in days gone by, to gaze at with an uncomfortable and suspicious look from having heard that always on Midsummer Eve, just at midnight, a number of skeletons started up from its roots, and joining hands, danced round it till cock-crow, and then as suddenly sank down again. My informant knew several persons who had actually seen this dance of death, but one young man in particular was named to me who, having

been detained at Findon by business till very late, and forgetting that it was Midsummer Eve, had been frightened (no difficult matter we may suspect) out of his very senses by seeing the dead men capering to the rattling of their own bones.'

I am sure that Broadwater is a very lively place full of lively people, but I hope they will forgive me if I once more refer to its churchyard. It was here that two of England's greatest nature writers are buried, Richard Jefferies and W.H. Hudson.

Jefferies was born in 1848 in Wiltshire, and lived there for the first thirty years of his life. From there he moved to Surrey, and it was only in the final years of his life that he discovered Sussex. None of his many books are specifically about Sussex, although some of the later ones refer to it. He wrote many books which are now classics of their kind including *Wild Life in a Southern County, Nature near London, Bevis* and *The Story of my Heart.*

Hudson was born in Argentina in 1841, and did not come to England until he was 32. In 1899 he spent the summer in Sussex with the intention of writing a book on the South Downs. In September, while living in the house in Goring where Richard Jefferies had died, he began writing *Nature in Downland.* It was published in 1900, and as well as dealing with natural history as his previous books, also included much on the people of the Sussex downland region. When he died, he joined his wife in Broadwater churchyard, and these words were inscribed around the grave:

'He loved birds and green places and the wind on the heath, and saw the brightness of the skirts of God'.

Bucks Green ✤

Named after Richard Buck, a local landowner of the 18th century, Bucks Green with Rudgwick really forms one village. The former lying along both sides of the A281 Horsham to Guildford road, and Rudgwick hiding itself on the secondary

B2128 road to Cranleigh. The two are inextricably combined in most of their activities. For instance the annual Rudgwick Fete, with its parade of decorated floats and Miss Rudgwick riding in a beautiful open horse-drawn carriage, takes place on the Rudgwick recreation ground behind the Rudgwick Village Hall; which is in Bucks Green!

Bucks Green evidently enjoyed its November 5th celebrations in the early part of this century. I have a wonderful photograph from this period showing a very respectable bonfire surrounded by a proud bunch of village men, and surmounted by a 'guy' in frock coat and top hat, holding a placard reading 'The Budget'. Evidently Guy Fawkes that year was supplanted by the Chancellor of the Exchequer; which seems to me to be a brilliant idea. One lady looking at the photography for the first time exclaimed 'there's my grandfather standing beside the bonfire'.

A local 'character', Percy Naldrett, lived and worked in Bucks Green as a printer, poet, conjuror, book collector and motor cyclist. He had been a friend of Hilaire Belloc, and like this great writer had a passionate love of Sussex. He drove through the country lanes of the county on his motor cycle, and one story was told of how when nearly 80, he carried his sister who was around the same age, on the pillion. It was said that this was the largest number of years ever seen on one motor cycle.

He worked as a printer in a tin shed within his garden, charging low prices and giving old world courtesy. He had been a member of the Magic Circle, and even up to the age of 82 visited a local school to perform his tricks to the delight of the pupils.

Four months before he died, he wrote a poem on his 85th birthday, which symbolised his great love of Sussex, and this was read at his funeral in Rudgwick Parish Church. It began:

'Farewell dear Sussex, the place that gave me birth,
Farewell to my beloved Downs,
Farewell to golden Weald with jewelled earth,
With snuggling inns and lovely ancient towns'.

39

Burpham 🙟

Some Sussex villages have a tremendous wealth of history and folklore, quite disproportionate to their size or importance. Burpham is surely one of them, in spite of its smallness and comparative inaccessibility.

The church of St. Mary is a little gem; mainly 12th and 13th century, restored in the 19th century with a sympathetic hand. There is a leper's window through which the poor victims of this disease who dwelt in a leper colony were blessed by the priest inside the church. There is even a leper's path or walk across Perry Hill to what is now Lee Farm. Another very unusual feature is an earth rampart, which according to tradition was built by the Saxons against Danish pirates. Here there is a 'Jacob's Ladder' or as it is known locally the 'Seventy Steps', which again tradition tells us was used by the smugglers when coming from the river to the pub with their brandy and silks.

In the churchyard is the grave of the Rev. Edward Tickner Edwards, who died at 79 in 1945. He was appointed Vicar of Burpham in 1927, holding the post until he retired in 1935, although he still continued to live in the area. He must have loved the place, as he originally came to live there from London, with his wife and young family; working as a writer, until at the age of 50 he joined the army in 1915. He started as a private, serving throughout the Gallipoli campaign, and ended the war as a captain. He was ordained in 1920, working at Lyminster and Folkington, before returning to his beloved Burpham in 1927.

Undoubtedly he was held in high regard as a cleric, and well loved by his flock, but it was as a writer that he found greatest fame. He wrote about the natural history and local lore of his village and its surroundings, and also about honey bees – one of his great passions. He also wrote several novels, with titles which mean nothing to most of today's readers, but which at the time were highly regarded. *Tansy* which he wrote in 1914 was made into a silent film in the 1920s and shown in over 16,000 cinemas. It starred Alma Taylor, a big name in her day. It was made in the Burpham area, which in the story is called Goldringham. A local shepherd, James Oliver, recalled how he worked his sheepdog out of sight of the camera, so that the star who played a shepherdess appeared to be the one controlling the dog.

As a writer on natural history, Tickner Edwards has been compared with Hudson and Jefferies, although his works never achieved the prominence of those two authors. His book *The Lore of the Honey Bee* (1908) has become something of a classic of its kind, and many people will have heard of it without knowing anything about the author.

An intriguing account of the ancient custom of beating the bounds as it was carried out at Burpham in 1810, appeared in the *Sussex County Magazine* for March 1936. It must have been a very thorough perambulation of the parish by the vicar, the churchwardens and other members of the congregation, with frequent stops for prayers, for marking out a cross and for eating and drinking. In fact the latter seems to have been a very important part of the proceedings, with 23 gallons of ale, several gallons of bread and cake, and an unknown amount of cheese being consumed by probably a relatively small number. A number of those present signed their name on a certificate following the 'beating', including the vicar, churchwardens, 'boys' and the parish clerk; who made his 'mark'.

Burpham's best known eerie tale is about Jack Upperton's Gibbet. The crime for which Jack was hanged in 1771, was attempted robbery of mail, which was being carried by William Baldry either to or from Steyning. There were two men in the hold-up, and local men have always believed that the real culprit got away, and Jack refused to turn informer. The vicar visited Jack Upperton in jail, and Jack told him 'It was a scrambling sort of turn-out'. When he was sentenced to death at East Grinstead, the judge Baron Perrett, pronounced 'Let him be hung in chains on the most convenient spot on Burpham New Down....' This was the custom of the time, and was evidently intended to deter other would-be wrong-doers. The blacksmith received £5 for making the irons and chains, which surely must have seemed a very grisly task. Legends and stories soon grew up around the gibbet, and the unfortunate man's bones were said to be still rattling two years after the execution. Although there appears to be no well documented ghost story, folk talk about Jack Upperton's ghost, and many have felt uneasy when visiting the site. There is a story told in differing versions, about a stranger who was being shown the gibbet, and at the same time being told that the ghost of the last highwayman had been seen there. A local wag who was in hiding then shouted 'and here he is' at the crucial moment. Collapse of stranger, as Punch might have said!

One man who knew a lot of stories about Jack Upperton, was the late Lawrie Graburn of Burpham, who wrote in the *West Sussex Gazette* under the name Newall Duke. He had a wonderful memory and a vast knowledge of country matters, so that all his stories were based on fact. 'Duke' was a family name and one of his relations who was a farmer, is said to have remarked to the Duke of Norfolk, 'You became a Duke by inheritance, your Grace, but I was born a Duke'.

One more story of old Burpham, as told by a contributor to the *West Sussex Gazette* in 1980. It was about the doctor who arrived to see a patient at night, on horseback and with a lantern to guide him. The doctor diagnosed bronchitis – the treatment brown paper across the chest, well covered with goose fat. And it worked!

Bury

Many Sussex villages have been fortunate in possessing a resident who had the energy and talent to record the history and local lore of the place for posterity, usually with little chance of monetary reward. *All about Bury* by Lillian E. Brown was originally put together as a Women's Institute *Village Record* (in 1932 the W.I. Federation suggested to village institutes that they should compile local histories). Over the years Miss Brown added to her collection of facts and reminiscences, and in 1948 it was published by a Hove bookshop, selling at ten shillings and sixpence. It is everything a local history should be; detailed and yet highly readable, and written with such an obvious love of the subject – the village of Bury. Nothing is too insignificant to escape Lillian Brown's notice. For instance we are told the gallery in the church of St. John, which was removed in 1900, was painted a mottled yellow with supporting pillars of brilliant blue – rather like a farm wagon. Boys liked to sit up there during the service, especially at Christmas time, as they could eat oranges and crack nuts undetected. The official church history tells us about the gallery, but not what colour it was, or about those boys!

Lillian Brown died in 1966, her little book remaining as a fitting memorial to her. On her death, the *West Sussex Gazette* commented that she always seemed to have a copy by her, to give to anyone interested, and it was doubtful if she ever made any money out of it. Although I knew of her book, I had not managed to find a copy once it had gone out of print, even by advertising for it. Then suddenly I came upon not one, but three copies, in a Brighton secondhand book shop. I hope the other two purchasers were as appreciative as I was.

An old Sussex riddle asked 'Where was beer sold by the pound?', the answer being 'In Bury – as the village beer house kept by Nancy Green, was next to the village pound'. Bury seems to have been blessed with enterprising ladies. In 1796, so we are told, the married women of Bury beat the single women in cricket by 80 runs, and then joined forces with them to challenge any other team of women in the country. And that's not all; in 1791 two Bury ladies with the names of Big Ben and Mendoza, took part in a prize fight before a large audience, with Big Ben the victor.

Bury lies across the river from Amberley, and until quite recent times there was a regular ferry, with at one time a ferrywoman – Mrs. Shepherd, who had taken over from her husband. In turn, she was replaced by her daughter, Mrs. Marshall.

But not all Bury ladies were so praiseworthy. Mrs. Latham in her *Some West Sussex Superstitions lingering in 1868,* talks of a cunning woman of Bury, who would tell young men or maidens whether their future spouses would be short or tall, rich or poor and dark or fair. She had heard of three young girls in their Sunday best, walking a long distance in order to consult the Bury 'witch'.

For local funerals, bearers once carried the coffin to Bury church. On one occasion having walked all the way from Westburton with their burden, the bearers left the coffin outside the pub while they went inside for some liquid refreshment. When funeral parties came across the fields between Westburton and Bury, it was the custom to place pennies on each set of gateposts the procession passed through. This was to show that no right-of-way existed, even if on this occasion permission had been given for the funeral party to use the route.

One of Bury's most famous residents was John Galsworthy, who lived at Bury House. Another Bury character was Mabel Constanduros, who some with good memories may recall from pre-war radio days, with her Buggins family. Although as far as I know, not a Sussex lady, Grandma Buggins certainly had her share of Sussex obstinacy. Mabel Constanduros lived at Prattendens Cottage, and she took a great delight in local affairs. She wrote the foreword to Lillian Brown's *All About Bury* in which she told of how she stayed at The Swan, Fittleworth, while she looked for a Sussex home, and fell in love with Bury. When she first saw 'Prattendens' she knew she had to have it. At that time there was no gas, electricity, main drainage or tap water in Bury, and she had to engage a dowser to help her find the right place for a well.

'Rather too remote' was one recent visitor's comment on Bury, but many will disagree. Lillian Brown found it very much to her liking, as this little poem from her enchanting book, shows:

'By Hill it nestles, calm and neat;
So old 'twas held in Saxon day,
By Countess Goda whom we greet,
In doomsday book; while next we meet,
The Norman Monks sent from their seat,
Of Fecamp Abbey to hold sway.

The Street full centuries has known –
So, too, the deep-cut Hollow Way,
The river busy trade did own;
O'er church eight hundred years have flown,
While Manor House, its ancient stone,
Could tell of Courts and justice shown,
And life as live in long-gone day.'

44

Charlton 🦋

This village was for many years very well known to the hunting fraternity. The Charlton Pack was once the most famous in the world, until it disappeared at the beginning of the 19th century. The most notable hunt in Charlton history took place on Friday January 26th 1738 and lasted from 8.0 am to 6.0 pm. The hunting members of the English aristocracy were there in force, although many dropped out during the day, and only three people were actually present at the death. The Duke of Monmouth so loved the hunting at Charlwood that he is supposed to have declared that 'when I become King of England I will come and keep my court at Charlton'.

In Charlton Forest, members of the infamous Hawkhurst Gang of smugglers met on Sunday October 4th 1747 to plan their raid on Poole Custom House, a crime which led eventually to the most famous trial in the history of southern English smuggling.

Arthur Beckett in *The Spirit of the Downs* (1909) tells of a legend concerning a pile of stones in Charlton Forest, which were known locally as 'The Smuggler's Table.' It was there that these gentlemen were said to hide their casks of spirits, although the stones were later removed.

The first official meeting of the first Women's Institute in England was held in the Fox public house in Charlton. A plaque recorded the event in these words:

> 'Singleton and East Dean W.I.
> On November 9th 1915
> The first Women's Institute
> meeting in England
> was held in this room'.

I feel that even if Charlton had no other claim to fame, this would still make it an important and historic place.

Chidham 🦋

Chidham's main claim to fame rests on the discovery of a new strain of wheat, the Chidham White. The Rev. Arthur Young in his *General View of the Agriculture of the County of Sussex* (1813) described it thus:

> 'As Mr Woods was occasionally walking over his fields, he met with a single plant of wheat growing in a hedge. This plant contained thirty fair ears, in which were found fourteen hundred corns. These Mr. Woods planted the ensuing year, with the greatest attention, in a wheatfield: the crop from these fourteen hundred corns produced eight pounds and a half of seed, which he planted the same year; and the produce amounted to forty-eight gallons: this he drilled, and it yielded fifteen quarters and a half, nine gallon measure. Having now raised a large quantity of seed, he partly drilled, and in part sowed, the last produce broadcast, over rather more than fifty acres of land, and he gained 38½ loads. Twenty loads of this quantity was sold for seed, at £15.15s. per load. The wheat, upon trial, was discovered to be so fine, that Mr. Woods had an immediate demand for a far greater quantity than he could spare for sale'.

Chithurst 🌿

A tiny village on the West Sussex-Hampshire border which Ian Nairn and Nikolaus Pevsner describe as 'lush and intricate in spring, like a Pre-Raphaelite picture'.

It once had its own tipteerer's play – the Sussex name for the traditional Christmas mummer's drama. Dorothy Marshall who lived at Chithurst House noted the play and others in the area, and encouraged their performance. This was in 1911, so the play evidently persisted well into the 20th century, and was possibly killed by the First World War, as were so many other traditional English things.

There is an excellent photograph of the Chithurst mummers in the Museum of English Rural Life at Reading, showing that there were seven players. They were F. Albery (Father Christmas), G. Stemp (Jolly John), J. Brown (Gallant Soldier), G. Brown (King George IV), E. Gardner (Turkish Knight), E. Hopkins (Noble Captain) and F. Dawtry (Doctor Good). They were almost certainly working men of the village, and the two Browns were probably related, as taking part in village plays was often a family thing.

The play was the normal hero-combat type, and the actors (apart from Father Christmas, who would have been more of a compere than a participant) carried swords painted with blue spiral stripes. Father Christmas had a holly-bush on a staff, similarly painted.

Gallant Soldier was dressed in a military uniform complete with medals, but the rest wore tunics and trousers covered all over with cut-out pieces of coloured cloth. Strips of coloured cloth hung from their clothes like ribbons, and their hats were well decorated with streamers and flowers. They must have looked a very merry sight.

Christ's Hospital 🎋

'C.H.' as it is so often called, is not actually a village, although it has roads and avenues, postal facilities, a chapel, a shop and a surprisingly large railway station. C.H. is the Blue-coat school of Christ's Hospital, founded in 1553 by Edward VI, and moved from Newgate in London to Stammerham, west of Horsham in 1902. Over 1,000 acres of green fields became a small town of large and small buildings, roads and sports areas. The red brick architecture has been critically commented on many times, but the remark by E.V. Lucas in *Highway and Byways in Sussex* (1904) that time might mellow the school, was wisely prophetic. Helped by the patina of eighty years, the tranquility of trees and lawns, and I suspect the acceptance of the familiar, the buildings have settled in quite comfortably. Several times I have had the pleasing experience of being shown round the school by one of the boys, dressed of course in the historic school attire of long dark blue coat, breeches and yellow stockings. The chapel provides quite a shock, with its sixteen almost too bright murals by Sir Frank Brangwyn; included is one of St. Wilfrid teaching the Sussex folk to fish.

The very distinctive uniform is a familiar sight in the streets of the neighbouring town of Horsham. Possibly something of a shock to visitors; almost like seeing beings out of English history. But residents do not notice even when a Christ's Hospital boy cycles past, with his long coat tucked up at the back, rather like a bustle, to leave his legs free. A group of Roman Catholic Christ's Hospital boys wearing their school dress in the 1930s took part each Sunday in the mass at St. John's Roman Catholic Church in Horsham, by processing on to the sanctuary carrying candle lanterns, just before the consecration and elevation of the Host, and remaining kneeling during this part of the service.

Christ's Hospital has many traditions, and much folklore of its own, and many books have been written giving the history of the school. It still maintains its strong links with the City of London, and the Lord Mayor makes his annual visit to the school on Speech Day. The fine Christ's Hospital band plays on occasions such as this, and also during school marches to chapel and to meals – and if this sounds very regimented, the answer is that there is no more efficient way of getting 850 boys from one place to another as quickly as possible. When the weather does not permit, then I am told the boys proceed to the dining hall by means of the useful underground passages, whch also carry all the water pipes, electricity cables and the like. Now Christ's Hospital has a modern Arts Centre, which is visited by audiences from a wide area, and has been televised many times.

Church Norton

A hamlet lying beside Selsey Harbour, with a tiny chapel said to have been built on the site of St. Wilfrid's original monastery. It was once larger, but in 1864 much of the material was used to build the parish church at Selsey, and only the chancel remains. A roughly carved monument of John Lewis and his wife Agnes, from 1537, remains.

Rudyard Kipling told the story of Eddi, a priest of St. Wilfrid, in a poem *Eddi's Service* in the book *Rewards and*

Fairies (1910). The time is midnight on Christmas Eve, and because the night is rough and stormy, none have come to attend midnight mass at the little chapel at Church Norton. But Eddi is determined to proceed with the service, saying 'I dare not shut his chapel, on such as care to attend'. And congregation there is, in the shape of an old marsh donkey and a yoke-weary bullock. I have seen it stated that the poem is based on a traditional manhood legend, but although Kipling loved Sussex folklore, I feel that this was most likely his own story. But whether traditional or not, it is a lovely story told in a lovely poem.

Clapham 🍂

An unpretentious village, the twin of Patching. The nice old church of St. Mary has a number of monuments of the Shelley family, including one with an epitaph worth quoting. This was how Sir John Shelley felt about his wife Wilhelmina, who was taken from him on 21st march 1772, at the age of 23.

'She was a pattern for the world to follow: such a being both in form and mind perhaps never existed before. A most dutiful affectionate and virtuous wife, a most tender and anxious parent, a most sincere and constant friend, a most amiable and elegant companion; universally benevolent, generous and humane; the pride of her own sex, the admiration of ours. She lived universally belov'd, and admir'd. She died as generally rever'd, and regretted, a loss felt by all who had the happiness of knowing her, by none to be compar'd to that of her disconsolate, affectionate, loving and in this world everlastingly miserable husband, Sir John Shelley.'

Poor Sir John!

Clayton

When two windmills stand close together they are usually known as Jack and Jill. In spite of the old Sussex countryman's joke , that there would not be enough wind for more than one mill in one place, it was not uncommon to find two together, although today the only twins left standing in Sussex are the much written about Jack and Jill on the Downs above Clayton village.

Jill, a white post mill, is quite an old lady, having been built in c. 1821. She stood originally in Dyke Road, Brighton, but as the town started to grow outwards, the buildings kept the wind away from Jill, and it was decided to move her to a more open position.

Jill arrived on the Downs in 1852, close to an older mill, known as Duncton or Duncton Gate Mill which had been built there in 1765. This mill no longer exists, although the roundhouse is still to be seen.

Jack, a brick tower mill, was built to replace the old Duncton mill in 1866, and Jack and Jill continued working in harmony until about 1907.

Mr Edward Martin, a writer and archaeologist, lived in Jack for three years and wrote of his experiences there in *Life in a Sussex Windmill* (1921). It is a fascinating account of what it is like to actually live in an old mill high up on the Downs, and he tells of his battles against slugs, mice, silverfish and so on. Alone at night, he wrote 'The silences were almost appalling'. But it was not always quiet. 'The mill in fact spoke. Sometimes there was a decided change of wind, and that rather suddenly. Then the groaning would be like a thousand demons let loose.'

Now there is a Jack and Jill Preservation Society, and it is hoped to return Jill to working condition and to turn Jack into a museum of Sussex mills and milling. One reason why it is important that the two mills should remain, is that they are good examples of the two distinct windmill types – the brick built tower mill, and the wooden post mill, the latter being the earliest type of windmill to be built in England.

Edward Martin, who lived in one of the mills, wrote of how he would watch the trains leaving Clayton railway tunnel at night, from his vantage point. The tunnel cost £90,000 to make, and is a mile and a quarter long. It was one of the many great engineering achievements, when the railway came to Sussex, and must have been a source of a great pride to the London, Brighton and South Coast Railway.

Unfortunately the tunnel is best known for the terrible accident which took place on Sunday 25th August 1861. Three trains were involved in a dreadful pile up, which was the result of the close proximity of the trains, compounded by errors made by overworked signalmen. Twenty three passengers died, and the *Illustrated London News* reported the scene in these horrified words: 'The engine of the third train had literally leaped upon the last carriage of the excursion train, completely smashing it, and then shivering the back of the next carriage to splinters. The two carriages contained sixty persons, who were all more or less mutilated, scalded or otherwise injured.' The accident was followed by a full scale enquiry by the railway company, and of course many claims for compensation. No doubt many lessons were learnt, at tremendous cost.

Clayton once had its tollgate, with the usual type of notice which began 'For every horse, mare, gelding, mule or other beast drawing any wagon, wain, cart or other such carriage...' Now the never-ending Brighton-bound traffic rushes close by, but when I spent a day in Clayton last year, I found it full of life and pride, determined to save its windmills and at the same time, its own village identity.

Climping 🦐

Or as some prefer to spell it, 'Clymping', is an attractive village, which becomes rather full of visitors on sunny summer days. The church of St. Mary is a little gem, described by most books on Sussex as both beautiful and interesting. An antiquary once used the phrase 'Bosham for antiquity; Boxgrove for beauty; and Climping for perfection'. Quite unusual to say something nice about one's own village, without at the same time denigrating the neighbouring ones.

An old rhyme listing the church bells of Sussex, begins; 'An old woman limping, says the bells of Climping'. But whether there ever was such a lady, or it merely made a good rhyme, we may never know. The church band once played regularly for services wearing white smock-frocks, and carrying their instruments and music in red handkerchiefs. Canon K.H. MacDermott commented that the white smocks were more in keeping with the grey old English churches, than the cassocks and surplices of the present day. (*The Old Church Gallery Minstrels.* 1948).

A correspondent in the *Sussex County Magazine* in 1936, asked what a small circular object like a sundial on the south side of the church tower represented. The answer given by the late Rev. A.A. Evans was that this was a mass or scratch dial, sometimes found on churches to help the faithful in times past attend at the correct time for the mass. Interestingly, a book of 1912 mentions this dial, but says it was probably a mason's mark; however, I feel sure Rev. Evans was correct.

An old tomb in the churchyard was supposed to have been used by smugglers for concealment of their contraband after it had been landed at the coast close by. Not at all unlikely, as this was very much smuggler's country, and we know that these gentry made use of any hiding places, either secular or sacred, when it suited them.

Lastly a lovely witch story, told by J. Wentworth Day in *Here are Ghosts and Witches* (1954). A Climping farmer was a very mistrustful man, and he used to spy upon his workmen from the top of a hayrick. One day, he was spotted by his men, and one of them who was a witch (witches can be either women or men in Sussex) said to his workmates 'I will soon cure him of this'. He bewitched the farmer, so that he could not move from the hayrick for two days, saying when he finally let him down 'perhaps you won't spy on us again'.

Cocking ✥

Cocking, or as the locals used to pronounce it 'Kokkun', is in a gap in the Downs on the Midhurst to Chichester road. A number of the buildings are owned by the Cowdray Estate, so the woodwork is painted a cheerful yellow, a colour apparently beloved of the Estate painters. The country around is well wooded, and there is a pond with the unlikely name of

Bumblekite. An unusual natural phenomenon seen in the neighbourhood used to be known as 'Foxes-Brewings'. This was a mist in the trees which was supposed to foretell rain if it rolled westwards towards Cocking.

Cocking had its own mumming or tipteers play, in which Father Christmas plays a slightly more prominent part than in most of these plays. It opens with the usual entrance speech from Father Christmas, and then the oddly named Mince Pie fights with St. George. The former is killed, and Father Christmas calls for a doctor, and he appears. Father Christmas bargains with him, and eventually the doctor gives in to the extent of reducing his fee by one farthing. The doctor then exclaims:

> 'I have a little bottle by my side,
> The fame of which spreadeth far and wide,
> The stuff therein is called Hallecumb pain.
> It will rise the dead to life again-
> It will cure the Hipsey Pipsey Paulsey and the gout,
> Pains inside and pains out.
>
> Drop a drop on the poor man's nose.
> Arise, young man, and show the gentle folks around,
> What a noble doctor there is to be found.'

The very abbreviated play ended with a further character, Little Saucy Jack, winding things up with this closing speech:

> 'In comes I little Jack,
> With all my family at my back,
> Christmas comes but once a year,
> And when it comes it brings good cheer:
> Roast beef, plum pudding and mince pies,
> Who takes all these things better than I?
> Christmas fairs makes us dance and sing,
> And money i' purse is a capital thing.'

Coldwaltham 🦋

A small village, completely ignored by many Sussex books. There are a number of nice old cottages and houses in the neighbourhood, and the church of St. Giles, which has a yew tree in the churchyard reputed to be 1,000 years old.

Many people will know the countryside hereabouts through staying at the West Sussex County Concil conference centre, Lodge Hill, where educational courses have been held for many years. A second generation of youngsters are now attending courses, following in the footsteps of their parents who went there in the 1930s and 1940s.

The Coldwaltham Parish Council was in the news in 1979 when a row erupted over who was responsible for animals straying on to the road, from the traditional 'Long Acre' – the grazing land beside the road from Coldwaltham to Greatham. Police had refused to prosecute because of confusion over the responsiblility for upkeep of the fences. The trouble blew up when about sixty cattle escaped and went on the rampage through the village. The Parish Council felt that the owners of the animals were the ones breaking the law.

Colgate 🦋

It has been said, rather unkindly, that Colgate is one of those villages that you can easily miss as you pass through it. No doubt the residents would disagree. Certainly the German Air Force didn't miss it on the night of September 10th 1940, when bombs fell on the District Nurse's cottage and on the Village Hall next door. Nurse Hocken was killed, as were three firemen. A third bomb hit the Post Office, but luckily the family had taken refuge in the woods. Yet another bomb went off the following morning, but without further injury or loss of life.

Thus Colgate lost its Village Hall in most tragic circumstances, but on May 30th 1958 a new Memorial Hall was opened – the work on it having been carried out by voluntary labour. When it was obvious that the cost of a new building was quite beyond the resources of the village, a call went out for local craftsmen to give their time and expertise. Although some thought the enthusiasm would not last, the building quickly grew and even the curtains for the windows were made by labour freely given. The clock on the outside of the hall was donated by the children of the village, who raised the money by making things to sell, and holding sales. The inscription on the hall reads 'This hall is dedicated to the Men and Women of the village of Colgate who died for their country during the 1939-45 World War'.

Colgate church (St. Saviour) is only just over 100 years old – it was consecrated on November 22nd 1871, having cost a little over £1,800 to build. Although relatively new as churches go, it incorporates an old chapel which stood on the same site.

Colgate is very much a part of St. Leonard's Forest, the last remaining wooded area of what was once known as Anderida. Legends abound, many of them connected with the forest around Colgate. Dragons and dragon slayers, lily beds from drops of blood, a dearth of nightingales and snakes, a smuggler who ran a race with the Devil (and won), the future King Charles II hiding in a yew tree on his flight to Brightenhelstone, white ladies, a black princess and a headless horseman. The latter was said to be Squire Powlett who for no known reason would leap upon the back of an unlucky horse with rider passing through the forest after dark. Such stories are not entirely things of the past. One lady told me quite sincerely of a headless figure seen by her husband near one of the furnace ponds in the forest, in quite recent times.

Perhaps the deer who inhabit the forest may be partly to blame for some of the eerie tales, or even the smugglers who were said to make frequent use of the wooded paths after dark. Mick Miles (or Mike Mills) was one of these gentlemen, and his mile-long avenue where he raced with the Devil may still be seen.

Compton 🦋

A pleasant downland village with a tiny square, near to the Hampshire border, and with a flint church (St. Mary) largely rebuilt in the mid-19th century. Not far away on Telegraph Hill is a fine prehistoric Long Barrow, 210 feet long, sometimes called Bevis' Thumb, and sometimes The Devil's Thumb.

Bevis, whilst a perfectly respectable Sussex giant was rather a literary hero, and it appears to me that the second name would be more acceptable to the average Sussex countryman. The Devil, under the name of Beelzebub, also featured in the traditional Compton Christmas play.

Early in this century the writer and founder of the *Sussex County Magazine,* Arthur Beckett, was looking for a village in Sussex where the 'tipteerers,' as the Sussex mummers were called, came out at Christmas time. After a search he discovered Compton, where the 'tipteerers' still held sway each year – in fact they offered to put on a special performance for him, as the Christmas season had passed. Quite rightly he refused to allow them to perform except at the proper time, and waited almost a year until the correct season. Much to the men's amazement he travelled nearly 60 miles to watch them perform their play, and he tells of this experience in his enchanting book *The wonderful Weald* (1911).

There were seven players, all dressed in curious costumes, except one who was the musician. The characters were Father Christmas, St. George, The Valiant Soldier, Little Johnny Jack, the Doctor and the Turkish Knight. On this occasion Beelzebub was missing, and his lines were spoken by Father Christmas.

The play opened in the time honoured way, by the Valiant Soldier:

> 'In come I, a roamer, a gallant roamer,
> Give me room to rhyme,
> I've come to show you British sport,
> Upon this Christmas time.
> Stir up your fire and give us a light,
> And see we merry actors fight.
> For in this room there shall be shown,
> The heaviest battle ever known.
> Betwixt St. George and the Turkish Knight.
> If you don't mind to believe these few words I've
> got to say,

56

Let the old gentleman slip in and clear the way'.
(The old gentleman was Father Christmas)

The action proceeded with St. George fighting and killing the Turkish Knight, the Doctor bargaining with Father Christmas before proceeding to bring the Turk back to life. Johnny Jack then adds a little comedy to the proceedings, before the Turkish Knight and the Valiant Soldier fight. Beelzebub concludes the play, calling himself Belsey Bob and begging the audience to contribute 'a halfpenny towards the rent a penny towards the grub'.

The tipteerers then sang their Mummer's Carol, a version of 'I saw three ships', followed by two other carols.

Here to conclude is a genuine piece of rustic humour from the Compton play; the Doctor is speaking:

'Look here, old gentleman; I had a man brought to me the other day; indeed he was not brought to me, he was wheeled to me in a left-handed wheelbarrow. He could not see anything without opening his eyes, and could not speak without moving his tongue.'

Coolham

Coolham is overlooked in many books on Sussex, and it is easy to feel that the world has passed it by. But once it was a hotbed of smuggling, and 100 years ago the village 'Club' was big enough to march with between 200 and 300 members and friends to an annual dinner in a marquee 90 feet long.

The most famous building in the vicinity is the quaintly named 'The Blue Idol', a Tudor farmhouse which includes the chapel or meeting house which William Penn founded in the 17th century for use by the Society of Friends, more commonly known as Quakers. It is still used for the same purpose today, and has been visited by people from all over the world including a Red Indian Chief whose ancestor made the original treaty of friendship with William Penn in America.

Many legends exist to account for the name. One is that the

house was repaired with timber taken from one of Penn's ships, and that a blue ship's figurehead was fixed to one of the gables; but no trace of such a figurehead exists. Until late in the 19th century the building appears to have been known as 'The Old House' so the name 'The Blue Idol' may be relatively modern.

Other conjectures include a story of pieces of blue pottery being found within the house; or that the building being untenanted at one time and being blue-washed, it was known as blue, and idle. Then there are those who believe that the name came from Celtic or Anglo-Saxon words. An even more unusual explanation is that the building was once a place of Roman Catholic worship, with a statue of 'Our Lady' wearing a blue garment.

Whatever the reason, it is one of the treasures of Sussex, and a reminder of one of the truly great men to have lived in the county.

Copthorne ✨

Copthorne is very much a border village, in fact it only just manages to be in Sussex by a whisker. In days gone by, prize fighting with bare fists took place here because it was so easy to slip across the county border one way or the other, depending on which body of police made an appearance. Copthorne had a reputation of being a place for fighting, and with a disregard for law and order. The men of the village were supposed to be rough and tough, and if a group of Crawley lads met a gang from Copthorne perhaps at a fair, there was sure to be a fight with the Copthorners almost certainly ending up as the victors. The village was the sort of place where a stranger didn't wander after dark, at least not if he was wise.

'Rough music' is an old custom which enabled villagers to show their displeasure at an unsocial act by a neighbour, although it is usually spoken of as having died out early in this century. However, it seems to have reappeared at Copthorne in the 1950s. In this case it was a man who had smacked his neighbour's son for hitting his daughter with a brick. The boy was taken ill soon afterwards, and his mother claimed that this was as a result of the chastisement meted out by the neighbour.

The boy's parents took the case to court, but to no avail, and apparently in desperation they persuaded some of their friends to join with them in providing 'rough music'. The usual collection of trays, pans, horns and so on was assembled and for three or four weeks, on a Saturday evening, the party paraded through the streets, ending up outide the culprit's cottage. Eventually the man and his wife took the hint, and moved away. It seems that even when an ancient custom such as this has completely died out, it can still surface almost spontaneously, and fill a social need.

A house in the village known as Smuggler's Cottage is pointed out as evidence of the prevalence of smuggling in this area. Justifiably so, in view of Copthorne's reputation for lawlessness and there is a story from the 1830s of one Jack Akehurst, who periodically at night would travel from Copthorne to Horsham, with his cart loaded with 25 two gallon casks or 'pigs' of smuggled spirits, and a supply of similarly acquired cigars.

George 'Pop' Maynard, Copthorne's grand old man in the 1950s, was well known as a local celebrity, a player of marbles and shove ha'penny, a singer and of course the oldest inhabitant. As a singer of traditional songs he became known to a wider circle than just his own friends, when he was broadcast by the BBC. The folk song series *As I Roved Out* included on one programme a recording of a party at the Cherry Tree, Copthorne, and George was the star singer.

Ken Stubbs, a dedicated folk song collector, made recordings of some of George's memories and these, together with some of his songs, are on tape in the Museum of English Rural Life, in Reading.

George was born in Surrey on January 6th 1832, but moved across the border to Copthorne, with his family, when still a boy. Apart from very short periods he lived there for the remainder of his life, dying at the age of 90 in 1962.

By trade he was a woodcutter, but like many countrymen, he turned his hand to other things when necessary. One other 'job' he did from time to time was poaching. He had no scruples, when his family was in want, in going out at night with his nets and coming home with a dozen rabbits, which could then be sold to the butcher for tenpence each. At that time poaching was rife among Copthorners, and an uncle of George's was known as 'The King of the Poachers'.

A very comprehensive little history of Copthorne has been compiled by J.H. Bentley, and is to be recommended.

Cowfold ❧

Hilaire Belloc wrote:

> 'They sell good beer at Haslemere,
> And under Guildford Hill;
> At little Cowfold, as I've been told,
> A beggar may drink his fill.'

Little Cowfold was not too far away from Belloc's Sussex home, and you may be sure the village was very familiar to him, and I am sure he was well aware of its charms. For it is a very charming village, with lots of nice cottages and a fine old church; St Peter's. In the church is a huge brass of Thomas Nelond, twenty sixth prior of St. Pancras, at Lewes, who died in 1433. It must be one of the largest church brasses in Sussex, and once brass-rubbers came from far and wide, but in recent times their attentions have had to be curtailed as the monument was suffering.

The churchyard fence has the names of village families on sections, showing who was responsible for the different parts of the sacred ground.

In 1657 the people of Cowfold were given the opportunity to elect a new vicar, although they really had little choice in the matter. Margaret Castock, a Quaker lady, tried to assert her rights and objected to the proposed minister on the grounds that he was unsound and corrupt in life and doctrine. For her pains she was taken before a magistrate and committed to Horsham gaol. Quakers were having a hard time in Sussex during this period, and were even thrown into gaol for such minor crimes as wearing a hat in church.

William Borrer, the ornithologist and author of *The Birds of Sussex* lived to the north of Cowfold, and must have noted down many of his birds in and around the village.

The pretty custom of May Garlands was encouraged in Cowfold early in the 20th century, and some photos I have show how the children of the village entered into the spirit of it. After all, if they worked hard at their flower garlands and chanted the old rhyme:

'The First of May is Garland Day, so please remember the Garland.
We don't come here but once a year, so please remember the Garland.'

then they could be reasonably sure of some useful pennies from indulgent grown-ups. The man who gave me the photographs is in one of them, as a young boy.

Visitors to the Cowfold area may be pardoned for thinking that there is another large church, or even a cathedral close-by. The lofty spire they can see belongs to the Carthusian Monastery known as Parkminster or St. Hugh's Charterhouse; or as it is most often called, Cowfold Monastery. It was founded in 1873, when the Carthusians were being expelled from France. It was designed to hold up to 80 monks, and in 1903 there were 50 brothers (30 of them priests) and 30 lay brothers. Now sadly their number is much smaller.

The monastery library has 20,000 volumes, but they have no radios, TV or newspapers. In the strange Sussex book *The Roadmender,* Michael Fairless refers to the Cowfold monks as 'The Bedesmen of St. Hugh'.

Crabtree

A little hamlet, south of Lower Beeding.

A story dating from 1799 is told by William Albery in *A Millennium of Facts* (1947) concerning the Crabtree Inn. A party of soldiers asked for something nice to eat at the inn, but nothing very appetising was forthcoming. As they were about to leave, one of the men was attracted by the loud singing of a canary in a cage. He asked the landlady the price of it, and although at first she refused to sell it, eventually she relented and quoted half a guinea. The soldiers paid over the amount, and took possession of the bird. They then wrung its neck, and demanded of the lady that it should be plucked and cooked. This was done, and the tiny meal was divided amongst them.

Cuckfield

Cuckfield

Although to many, Cuckfield (pronounced Cookfield) is now a small town, I am including it in this book of West Sussex villages, partly because I remember it when it definitely was a village, but also because there is so much of interest to write about it. Indeed I feel I ought to be writing a whole book about Cuckfield, and not just squeezing all the many things that come to mind into a few pages.

Historically it seems to have been a very busy place. An old Sussex character remarked 'This must be Cuckfield, there's houses on both sides of the street' and most people will sense exactly what he meant.

The church of the Holy Trinity is the focal point of the village, as it should be, and as is so often the case in Sussex. An old picture postcard from the days when the postage rate for a postcard was one old halfpenny, has a handwritten message on the back of the view of the church: 'In this dear old church I and my eldest sister and brother was christened. The house I was born in was at the front gate of the churchyard. I thought as you were collecting you would like this. One day I must get you an album like Aunt Aggie's, to keep them in'. I hope the young recipient appreciated the card, and eventually obtained his, or her, album.

An elaborate set of rules was drawn up in 1699, regarding the use of the gallery in the church. These stated that 'This gallery being built only for ye singing of Psalms by those yt have learnt, and for their singing ym together, therefore tis agreed that it be used by such only (and those allowed to be Good or Competent Singers by ye major part of the Quire) and by no other, tho' Proprietor, till approved singers'. There then followed instructions for the seating of everyone according to rank, with the women and maidservants yielding to their 'betters'.

Mrs Ann Pritchard Sergison, a member of a Cuckfield family, died in 1848 aged 85. She was known as 'wicked Dame Sergison' on account of her foul temper. After her death, ghost stories began to circulate about her – local people said she was too wicked to rest, and her spirit was supposed to have been seen swinging on the gate at the entrance to Cuckfield Park. After some time, three local clergymen were supposed to have held a service of exorcism in Cuckfield church at midnight. The story continued that the ghost was then drowned in the font, and the manifestations came to an end. Dame Sergison was not the only Cuckfield ghost by any means. There was also Geranium Jane, who was said to haunt a local pub.

Another story is of 'The Sleeping Maid of Cuckfield', and for this we go back to 15th September 1807, when a housemaid fell asleep in the attic bedroom of the house where she worked. The girl then slept continuously for eight days. When her employer called the village doctor, he could not account for her condition but reported that her body temperature had dropped. She awoke on 22nd September, having suffered no ill effects, and her story became just another Cuckfield legend.

Cuckfield is full of folklore. On St. Crispin's Day (25th October) it was one of the Sussex villages which celebrated with a bonfire, rather like Guy Fawkes Day. The boys went around blacked-up, asking for pennies, and as it was the Cobbler's feast day, it was the custom for shoemakers to give their employees a dinner in the evening. On Good Friday, often spoken of in Sussex as 'Marble Day', the game of marbles was played in the village churchyard in the 19th century – not as unusual as it sounds.

The *Sussex Weekly Advertiser* carried a story in 1797 concerning a curious wager accepted by a flax-dresser. He agreed to attempt to eat a square foot (about 42 pounds) of plum pudding in a fortnight. A number of bets were taken on the outcome. A week later the man was feeling a little sick, but eating about four pounds of pudding at his seventh meal, and varying the flavour with mustard and vinegar. But a day later his jaws refused to work any longer; he was forced to give in.

Andrew Boord, the original 'Merry Andrew' is supposed to have come from Borde Hill to the north east of Cuckfield. Some Sussex authors have claimed that Gotham in *The Merry Tales of the Mad Men of Gotham* which has been credited to Andrew Boord, was in fact Gotham, near Pevensey, in Sussex, and not the Nottinghamshire village of the same name.

Lucy Broadwood, the Sussex collector of folk songs, obtained some of the songs in her collections from Samuel Willett. He was known as 'the Singing Baker of Cuckfield', and he sent songs to Miss Broadwood through the post, as he was capable of writing musical notation accurately. Included in the songs she obtained from him was possibly the best known of all traditional songs collected in Sussex. *The Farmer's Boy.*

'The sun went down behind yon hill, across the dreary moor;
Weary and lame a boy there came, up to a farmer's door.
'Can you tell me if any there be that will give me employ,
To plough and sow, to reap and mow, and be a farmer's boy?
and be a farmer's boy?'

A song said to be particularly popular in Cuckfield was *Up to the Rigs of London Town*. In 1959 the magazine *Ethnic,* printed the words of a version of this song, as sung by Peter Gander and Bill Hawkes of Cuckfield, both then in their eighties.

'As I walked up London Street,
A pretty little gel I chanc't to meet,
Bein' oftentimes she did me greet,
With 'er poison'd darts an' 'er kisses sweet,
I was up to the rigs of London Town,
There was charmin' girls in London Town.'

The *Sussex County Magazine* of July 1954 printed a collection of memories from 'The Grand Old Man of Cuckfield', Mr William Edward Mitchell, who had just died in this 93rd year. These included tales of the old fair, the charter for which was supposed to have been granted in the 13th century. The booths stretched from opposite the Cuckfield clock down the street to Hoadley's Corner. Originally for cattle, it later became a pleasure fair. The stall holders were such a nuisance, restricting traffic and making holes in the road, that the charter was revoked about 1874. A site near the Kings Head was reserved for a boxing booth, and Mr Mitchell recalled seeing Tom Thumb exhibited in a booth opposite the bank.

Timothy Burrell was one of our Sussex diarists, although his diary entries were really intended as sidelights on his accounts. They show very well how a Sussex squire lived in the 18th century, although perhaps Timothy was not completely typical. It is clear that he was a kind-hearted, scholarly, old English gentleman, with a whimsical wit and some very human traits. He was born at Cuckfield in 1643, educated at Cambridge and became a barrister in London. In 1683 he succeeded to the family estates and lived from that time until his death in 1717, at the family seat of Ockenden House, Cuckfield. His diary includes lovely little hand drawn pictures of the things he was writing about – a new wheelbarrow; a bell given to him by his niece; two hats for his servants; and even Cuckfield church. He was a very benevolent character, and he loved inviting people to dine with him, particularly at Christmas, and he included the humbler members of society and not just his own class. The following is the fare provided at a dinner at Ockenden House on 1st January 1706:

> 'Plumm pottage, calve's head and bacon, goose, pig, plumm pottage, boiled beef, a clod, two baked puddings, three dishes of minced pies, two capons, two dishes of tarts, two pullets'.

But not all excitement in Cuckfield was in the past. The village declared itself independent in 1965 when there was an internal clash with the local Council. Rhodesia had recently declared U.D.I., and Cuckfield decided to do likewise, and so an independent state was born in Sussex. Now an annual mayoral election is held, and anyone can vote as many times as they like on payment of one penny a vote. In October 1983 the annual Independence celebrations were held for the 18th year, with Jimmy Swain the new mayor, having chalked up a total of 98,035 votes, in what must be the most corrupt election in the world. As usual the mayor rode in a carriage drawn by donkeys, with a pony escort. It is all great fun, and all done for charity.

Dial Post 🎜

A friendly little village, straddling the A24 on the way to Worthing. At least I found the members of the village W.I. very friendly when I visited them in the tiny village hall. The Dial Post (and West Grinstead) W.I. met on the first Thursday of each month, and instead of the customary excellent refreshments, they went one better with a sit-down meal at the end of the meeting – which I was assured was quite usual.

No church, no station, no gas mains, and of course no mention in most books on Sussex. But once it was a place known for smuggling activities, and there was also a village witch. The latter features in the following story. When a local man and his sons were bearing a coffin from the village to the churchyard at West Grinstead, the witch was seen to be following the little procession. Halfway there she declared that she would take a short cut, and disappeared, turning up again when they reached the church. Afterwards all the bearers agreed that the weight of the coffin had increased when they were apparently unaccompanied, and that it had suddenly become lighter when the old woman reappeared. They swore that she had made herself invisible and ridden on the coffin.

Dragons Green 🌿

This delightfully named little hamlet, close to Shipley, which is not far from Horsham, is said by some to be so called because of the dragon legends associated with St. Leonard's Forest.

The aptly named pub The George and Dragon, although tastefully modernised without spoiling its traditional charm, was once a beer house reached by a country lane. It has legends of smugglers, as well as the local dragon. Nowadays it serves snacks and lunches, and is a very popular hostelry with both the locals and visitors.

The tombstone outside the pub comes as rather a shock to strangers, although local people are now so used to it they don't give it a second glance. As may be expected there is a strange, and rather sad, story to account for it.

Around a century ago a boy called Walter Budd lived at the pub with his parents. He was an albino and an epileptic, and because of this he was shunned by most of the other boys. When he was accused of a minor theft, this proved to be the final humiliation, and he drowned himself.

The tombstone inscription reads 'In loving memory of Walter the Albino son of Alfred and Charlotte Budd. Born February 12th 1867. Died February 18th 1893. May God forgive those who forgot their duty to him who was just and afflicted'.

The vicar of the time, and some of his parishioners, objected to the final sentence, and Mr and Mrs Budd were asked to remove the tombstone from Walter's grave in Shipley churchyard. So to get their own back on the vicar and those who had slighted their son, the parents had the memorial re-erected in the front garden of their beer house, which because it was not owned by a brewery, they had every right to do. And there it has remained until this day.

What has been described as 'the good old Sussex game of Dwile Flonking' has been played in recent years in Dragons Green. The game is played by two teams of ten players. One team stands circling a beer barrel, with hands joined, whilst a player from the opposing team hurls the 'dwile' (a beer soaked rag) with a pole, trying to hit one of the team moving round the barrel. A point is scored when a player is hit. The game is apt to get a little out of hand rather quickly, and rules are broken or completely forgotten. It is great fun, but I have grave doubts about the antiquity of the game – in fact no one I have spoken to about it seems to have heard of it until about 20 years ago. But perhaps we are witnessing a new tradition in the making.

Duncton 🦡

Looking in my notebooks for material on the village of Duncton, I continually came across references to the old custom of wassailing the apple trees, which was carried on very energetically here until the 1920s. The captaincy of the Duncton Wassailers seems to have been handed down in the Knight family, the best known of the men who filled this post over the years being Richard 'Spratty' Knight.

On 'Old Christmas Eve' January 5th, they would call at local houses with orchards, blowing their horns and basic instruments made out of gas piping, and recite their chant:

> 'Here stands a good old apple tree
> (or Green Pippin tree or whatever),
> Stand fast Root.
> Bear well top.
> Every little bough.
> Bear apples now.
> Every little twig.
> Bear apples big.
> Hat fulls.
> Cap fulls.
> Three score, sackfulls.

Holler, boys, holler'.

Alternate lines were taken by the two halves of the group of wassailers, with the Captain shouting out the last line. After the ceremony, which was intended to frighten away any evil spirits that might be lurking in the branches of the trees, and to ensure a good crop of fruit in the coming season, the party would probably retire to the kitchen of the house for some refreshment.

Whilst wassailing, whostling or howling went on during the days following Christmas in most Sussex villages until the end of the 19th century, it seems that Duncton can claim to have had the longest uninterrupted record, carrying on well into the 20th century.

A photograph taken about 1897 showed the Duncton wassailers as they were at that time with Spratty, a handsome man with a bushy beard, resplendent in his costume. His wife was beside him holding a cake on a plate, and a jug, possibly containing cider. Spratty's son, William Knight (the vice-captain) stood beside him, also wearing a decorated hat.

The captain is holding a horn in the picture, which was a copper and brass hunting horn, bearing the inscription 'Thomas Bridger. Duncton Beagles. November 1860'. But information on the Duncton Beagles, or an explanation of how their horn became a prop for the wassailers, is completely lacking.

The church of Holy Trinity is comparatively modern, having been built in 1866, replacing an older one, St. Mary's, pulled down in 1876. The church still has an interesting bell, dated 1389, probably the oldest church bell in Sussex. The origin of the bell has puzzled experts, as the inscription appears to point to it being of Norman origin, although for a long time it was thought of as a Dutch bell.

A well known Sussex cricketer, James Broadbridge, was born at Duncton in 1796. It was said that he could do anything with a ball, except make it speak. To play in matches he would walk from Duncton to Brighton, looking more like a country farmer than a successful sportman.

Earnley 🦜

Earnley, or Erinleie as it was once called, was described some years ago as the most remote hamlet in the kingdom and also as being 'on the road from nowhere to nowhere'. Said perhaps in critical vein, but now something many other places strive after.

Earnley windmill has several claims to fame. In 1827 it was raised about seven feet, probably – and surprisingly – by jacking up the whole structure and adding brick courses one by one. It was certainly the last working windmill in Sussex carrying canvas on its sails, and it has also been claimed as the last full working windmill in the county; it ceased to function as such in 1946.

A correspondent to the *West Sussex Gazette* remembered when corn was delivered to the mill by a waggoner wearing a Sussex smock; and fresh bread was taken round the villages by horse and cart.

Eartham 🦜

A lovely, and still mercifully unspoilt downland village.

Eartham House was owned by the now unfashionable poet, William Hayley, who inherited it from his father. Although he was known as the 'Hermit of Eartham' he seems to have done a lot of entertaining, including in his guests many of the celebrities of the arts and literature of the time, including Cowper, Flaxman, Blake, Romney, Hurdis and Charlotte Smith.

His only son, who died at the age of 20, is commemorated in the church of St. Margaret, with a monument by Flaxman, which carries an epitaph written by his father. Hayley also wrote the funeral sermon.

Although possibly known chiefly as a poet, he was offered the Laureate – which he refused, he also wrote many prose works, and in addition seems to have delighted (if that is the right word) in writing epitaphs for the graves of his friends.

When Hayley moved permanently to his seaside home at Felpham, Eartham House was sold to the statesman William Huskisson, who was afterwards killed at the opening of the

Liverpool and Manchester Railway. There is a monument to him in the church.

On a lighter note, Eartham is commemorated in both song and story. The former as the name of a hymn tune, in a collection of Sacred Melodies by T. Bennett, a Chichester organist. (It was actually a melody by Rousseau, renamed for the purpose of the collection). In literature Eartham made its mark, although in the guise of 'Ashner', in a novel *Murder of the only witness* by J.S. Freeman.

Easebourne ෴

This is one of the Cowdray villages, sparkling with its bright estate-yellow paint. The church of St. Mary was formerly used as their chapel by a small order of nuns who lived in the nearby priory from c.1248. It has been suggested that this priory existed as a sort of reformatory for nuns of good families who had misbehaved. We do know that a visitation in 1441 brought to light many irregularities, particularly on the part of the Prioress who was stated to have lived and dressed in a far too worldly style. Her furs alone were valued at 100 shillings, and she was ordered to sell these in order to pay off some of the nuns' debts. In 1748 there was again scandal, and in 1535 the house was closed. Not surprisingly there is the usual legend of a tunnel from the nuns' priory, to Cowdray Park not far away. (The remains of the priory now form the vicarage for the church.)

Cowdray House took sixty years to build, and then was burnt down in 1793, existing today as a grand ruin. The legend of the 'Cowdray Curse' is well known, although experts have tried to prove that it never actually existed. Most people believe that the origin of the curse dates from the time when Sir Anthony Browne turned the monks out of Battle Abbey, in order to live in it himself. The last monk to leave the abbey solemnly declared that Sir Anthony's line would perish by fire and water. In 1793 the house succumbed to fire, and shortly afterwards the 8th Viscount was drowned. Two further male members of the family met their deaths by drowning in 1815. An alternative version of the legend places it within the context of the suppression of Easebourne Priory, making the nuns rather than monks responsible.

Another tunnel legend says that a secret passage existed from the village pub, and was used by smugglers. The village was described to me as a hotbed of smuggling, even up to relatively modern times. Illicit goods were carried across the Downs tied underneath sheep, and passed from one shepherd to another. An old man who lived in the village, and died about 50 years ago, boasted that he had killed an excise man and buried him on the Downs. This took place when the officer tried to take the man's brother prisoner, after catching him in the act. After the old man's death, a pair of breeches with a long dark stain down one leg, were found hidden in a cupboard. As these were much too small to have fitted the householder, it was supposed that they had belonged to the murdered excise man.

Eastergate 🌿

An old Sussex bell rhyme includes the following immortal lines:

> 'I'll give you a slap on the pate,
> Says the bells of Eastergate'.

But why the bells of the village should be so belligerent, I have been unable to find out. Perhaps they just couldn't think of a better thyme for Eastergate.

The murals, many painted by Byam Shaw, in the village hall, are well known and have been written up in several Sussex books. Arthur Mee in his *Sussex* (1937) was particularly enthusiastic about them, calling the collection 'one of the finest art collections possessed by any village in Sussex'. The hall which houses the pictures was built originally for use by the Territorial Army, and this has also attracted very complimentary comments.

The murals, which are all of Sussex scenes, depict St. Wilfrid landing at Selsey; King Harold hunting wild boar in local forests; Queen Elizabeth I at a deer shoot in Cowdray Park in 1592; Arundel Castle at the time of the Civil Wars; the flight of the future King Charles II through Sussex; the Sussex cricketer Dick Newland, who lived at Slindon; a regiment of

Dragoons on the march; the Sussex author, John Selden; and Romney sketching novelist Charlotte Smith in the grounds of Eartham House. The latter was a disappointment to author Hardiman Scott, who found it to be painted in murky greys and greens, with none of the figures very plain. Presumably he might be more satisfied today, as in 1977 Pagham picture restorer Arthur Baker and Eastergate painter Dennis Frost began the task of restoring the murals to their original bright colours.

East Preston 🦡

The church of St. Mary the Virgin dates from the 12th century with an added 19th century aisle. It has a stone spire, one of the very few in the county, and a stone porch.

Tipteering, the Sussex name for mumming, was revived in East Preston in 1911 by a Mr Foard, who was then about 40. As a boy he had been one of a gang which an old man named Barnard sent out on November 5th as bonfire boys, and at Christmas as mummers. Any money they collected he kept, rewarding the boys with sweets.

The revival team prospered for several years, until it was killed by the First World War. They went out each Christmas time, walking from one big house to the next, and sometimes bewildering pioneer motorists, when a Father Christmas and a motley group of characters appeared on a country lane. After they had performed their play, they were suitably refreshed and it needed considerable strength of will to remain sober enough to get through the evening. Christmas Eve was always reserved for performances in their own village.

The sign of the Roundstone Inn at East Preston has a grim story attached to it, or perhaps it would be more accurate to say several possible stories. The sign shows on one side a large round stone rolling down a hill, and on the reverse the stone is lying at the foot of the hill with a skeleton crushed beneath it.

The commonest story to account for the sign is that a wrongdoer or a suicide was buried at the crossroads, and because of the possibility of the deceased haunting the neighbourhood, a millstone was placed upon the body and a stake driven through the hole in the centre of the stone, and through the heart of the unfortunate beneath. This is of course in accord with the treatment which was meted out to suicides in rather less englightened times.

A slightly less grisly story says that the roundstone was the grinding stone from the windmill on Highdown Hill which was blown down during a bad storm. One of the stones smashed its way through the side of the mill, rolling down the lane leading from the mill to the main road. Here a farm worker on his way home was struck by the stone and killed.

The artist who designed and painted the original sign was Mr Ralph Ellis, who came from Arundel and was a very well known inn-sign artist in Sussex.

Ebernoe ⧉

It seems that Ebernoe has long had a reputation for remoteness. Not merely in the geographical sense, but because the village has not wished to become too firmly a part on the modern world. In 1938 *The Times* reported that the small population, with a few exceptions, paid little heed of British Summer Time. Mind you, it would not have been too difficult to find quite a lot of Sussex villagers who still lived by 'God's time', even well into the 1930s.

Perhaps I should not even refer to Ebernoe as a village, as there is so little of it. No pub, no shops, and just a very small church, Holy Trinity, built in 1867. Nairn and Pevsner (*The Buildings of England. Sussex.* 1965) call Ebernoe 'An improbable, enchanted place in the middle of the weald with an air of never having been touched by the twentieth century'. The church they dismiss as 'A tiny box-of-bricks chapel'.

But once a year Ebernoe picks up its trim 19th century skirts and really comes alive. This is July 25th (St. James' Day), when Horn Fair is celebrated on the Common. Surprisingly for such a tiny place, two or three thousand people have been known to attend the fair on a good year, the main event of which is a cricket match between Ebernoe and a neighbouring village. The culmination of the day is the presentation to the highest scorer of the horns of a sheep which has been roasting nearby all day.

The fair is said to be centuries old, although nobody knows exactly how many centuries. There is definite evidence of a revival in 1864 after a lapse of a great many years. Since then it has continued, with a few breaks and revivals.

The folklore aspect of the fair is particularly interesting. The name must allude to an ancient custom of dressing up with horns as a symbol of cuckoldry. Country humour was once rather basic, and subjects such as seduction and cuckoldry would have been fair game for jokes right up to the 19th century.

An old saying 'All's fair at Horn Fair' points to the supposition that Horn Fairs (and there were others) had a reputation for rough and wild behaviour; although all is decorum at today's fair at Ebernoe.

There is a tradition of thunderstorms on Fair Day, and a storm means good luck and good crops in the coming season. No storm, means the opposite. Another pleasant tradition is that gardeners are reminded to sow their spring cabbages on Ebernoe Fair Day.

An account in the *West Sussex Gazette* of the 1864 Horn Fair includes the following atttractive example of 19th century reporting:

> 'One of the most conspicuous objects of interest was the roasting of the horned sheep in the open air. A large group was gathered and notwithstanding the intense heat could not tear themselves away from the seething and sputtering object of their admiration. In another part of the ground an exciting match of cricket between Ebernoe and Plaistow was taking place. The large booth of Mr A. Puttick, landlord of the Stag, was brimming full of delighted spectators. Many a lusty pot of ale ran down the throats of the jovial company in honour of this glorious revival. As the sun descended below the horizon two bands struck up enlivening airs, which was the signal for tripping it on the light fantastic toe.'

One is tempted to add 'and so we say farewell to glorious Ebernoe for another year', but perhaps that would be unkind to the unknown reporter.

The cricket field is bisected by the road, and although traffic is light, a cricketer friend has regaled me with stories of games being held up at crucial moments by the sight of a car approaching, which none of the players recognise, and therefore no one knows whether the driver will stop or drive gaily on.

The Sussex Trust for Nature Conservation owns 175 acres of Ebernoe's Common, which was purchased in 1980 for £90,000. Included is the old hammer pond, and the site of the old Ebernoe brickworks, now an official ancient monument. The works, including a kiln and a moulding shed are in the woods, and had been in use for around 250 years when they finally closed down in the 1930s.

Edburton 🦢

Edburton's 13th century church of St. Andrew is said to have been founded by Alfred's granddaughter. It is the little grey church in Michael Fairless' strange Sussex book *The Roadmender*, and it has a rare lead font; once used as a horse trough, before being rediscovered and restored to its rightful place and purpose.

A beautiful description of a 19th century service in the church appears in Nathaniel Paine Blaker's *Sussex in Bygone Days* (1919). 'The Parish Clerk sat behind a desk on the same level as the floor. The congregation sat in high pews, ranged on each side of the aisle, east of the pulpit, in which they could repose comfortably without fear of observation, while on the west side of the pulpit and on each side of the aisle was a row of free seats on which the rest of the congregation sat, the men on one side and the women on the other. The service was performed by the Parson and Clerk, each reading a verse alternately in the psalms, and the Clerk saying Amen at the end of the prayers; the congregation, many of whom could not read, not joining in the responses. The hymns were sung by a choir, consisting of eight or ten men of the village, who sat in a pew

76

with a desk in the centre, and were accompanied by a bass viol, flute and all kinds of music. They took great pleasure in their performance and frequently met at each other's houses for practice.'

Almost every Sussex village has some story of smugglers or smuggling, and Edburton is no exception. Early in the 19th century, most of the villagers were frightened to go near a large wood, as a ghostly animal, the size of a calf with flaming eyes, had been seen there. One man, more daring than the rest, braved the ghost and discovered a cache of smuggled goods. Not the first time smugglers had enlisted the aid of ghostly spirits to hide their own more substantial ones.

Faygate ✑

A rhyme about the bells of Sussex says 'Hurry up, or you'll be late, say the bells of Faygate'. But sad to say, Faygate has no bells. Neither has it treacle mines, although another old Sussex saying credits it with that useful industry.

Once it must have had a 'gate', and it would be nice to believe in the suggestion of a correspondent to a Sussex newspaper in 1960, that the name should be 'Fey-gate' or the gate on the edges of St. Leonard's Forest where the fairies meet. He even suggested that the parish council should erect a sign showing a gate with fairies seated on it.

Whether Faygate once had fairies or not, it certainly had a widow who claimed to have seen the locally famed St. Leonard's Forest dragon. The account which was actually published and sold in London in 1614 had the following memorable title:

True and wonderful, a discourse relating to a strange monstrous serpent or dragon, lately discovered, and yet living to the great annoyance and divers slaughters both of men and cattle by his strong and violent poyson, in St. Leonard's Forest, and thirty miles from London, this present month of August, 1614, with the true generation of serpents.

The truth of the tale was vouched for by John Steele,

Christopher Holder and 'a widow woman dwelling at Faygate'. The dragon was stated to be nine feet or more in length and shaped almost in the form of an axle-tree. It had black scales along its back and red scales under its belly. It was said to be very proud and arrogant, with two great bunches on either side which it was supposed might be incipient wings. The reptile killed with venom, as its victims were poisoned but not preyed upon in any way. It was supposed to cover an area of between 3 or 4 miles, but was often seen at Faygate.

My own particular memory of Faygate is a much more modern one, relating to the period of the 2nd World War when I was a teenager. Faygate's notable contribution to the war effort was to house a small RAF unit. They were accommodated in huts, with a hangar type building – but no planes. In fact the site was probably much too small for aircraft, and I am unsure what role they were fulfilling, although I am sure it was a useful one. I visited the camp one evening to report for the local newspaper on a revue which the airmen and women were providing for the locals. I was deputising for a friend, a junior reporter, who was covering an event elsewhere. They treated me as a seasoned representative of the press (which I was not) and I treated them as experienced performers (which they were not). As I recall the show was not particularly good, but I gave them a tremendous write-up, and everyone was satisfied.

Felpham ✍

> 'Come in and welcome,
> Says the bells of Felpham,'

Thus the old bell rhyme sets the tone of this charming, welcoming village. I first made its acquaintance when, as a young teenager on a cycle, I explored the coastal villages in this area of Sussex. Although the barbed-wired beach was not far away, and there was a little wartime factory in the main street, it still seemed incredibly quiet and peaceful, and indeed unwarlike.

Many people will be familiar with Felpham through its association with the two literary figures, William Blake and

William Hayley. Blake called the village 'the sweetest spot on earth', and his beloved cottage still stands in Blake's Lane. Hayley wanted Blake to do the engravings for his proposed biography of Cowper. In 1800 Blake moved into his cottage at half past eleven one night. To start with all was idyllic, but after a time he chafed at Hayley and his titled friends, and after three years he returned to London and the life he knew best. But his Sussex period, while it lasted, was a fairly happy one. While he was at Felpham he had a vision of his dead father and brothers when he was walking to Lavant. He also 'saw' a fairy funeral, describing the little people as being of 'the size and colour of green and grey grasshoppers, bearing a body laid out on a rose leaf, which they buried with songs; and then disappeared'. It was here also that he wrote the lines which later became immortalised as *Jerusalem* – sung at thousands of W.I. gatherings throughout the years.

The one incident which really marred his time in Sussex has been recounted many times. Blake's gardener had invited a soldier, John Scholfield, to help him in the garden. Blake did not know of this arrangement, and seeing a stranger in his garden, asked him to leave. The soldier became bellicose, whereupon Blake took him by the elbows and escorted him out. Scholfield was not a nice character and plotted his revenge. He accused Blake of sedition and the magistrates had to hear the case, but of course Blake was acquitted.

In a poem which he wrote to Mrs Anna Flaxman, he summed up his feelings for Felpham:

> 'Away to sweet Felpham, for Heaven is there;
> The ladder of angels descends through the air;
> On the turret its spiral does softly descend,
> Through the village then winds, at my cot it does end.'

Blake's reputation is secure – as a poet, artist and visionary. Hayley's is rather less so.

He did have a special knack with epitaphs, which he seems to have enjoyed writing. This is one of the nicest, which he wrote for a Felpham blacksmith:

'My sledge and hammer lie reclined;
My bellows too have lost their wind;
My fire's extinct; my forge decay'd,
And in the dust my vice is laid;
My coal is spent, my iron gone;
The nails are driven – my work is done.'

To end, a strange story about Felpham, as told by the late Gerard Young in *The Cottage in the Fields*. (1945). A family lived in a cottage on church ground, and the vicar wanted it pulled down. The mother resisted, but one day the demolition men arrived and began their work when the family were eating their meal. The mother was naturally very upset, and feared for the safety of her children. She fetched the vicar, and argued with him, but he was adamant. She quietly said 'One above will remember you for this'. The family moved away, and years later returned to Felpham. As they passed the church, the parson came out, being helped along, as he had become almost paralysed. As the pitiful figure passed by, the mother looked at him and said 'God did not forget you'.

Fernhurst

Friday's Hill House at Fernhurst, once a regular meeting place of the Fabian Society when it included George Bernard Shaw and the Webbs, has a ghost story attached to it, concerning a parlour maid seen by the family living there in the 1900s. Guests at a dinner party in 1904, saw and commented separately on this household servant from the spirit world, but I have not heard of any explanation to account for this particular apparition.

One would expect Fernhurst to be peopled by ghosts from the days of the Sussex ironworks, as the history of the village is closely linked to this industry. Alice M. Tudor who wrote a comprehensive and factual history – *Fernhurst: the story of a Sussex village* (1969) said in her introduction 'Fernhurst was never a Black Country, but for two hundred years the noise of the hammers of the ironworks disturbed its peace and the felling of the woodlands robbed it of much of its beauty'. Although all that is very much in the past, many of the names linking the area with the old iron foundries remain. For example Furnace Pond, Furnace Wood, Ironhill Common, and Minepit Copse.

The old spelling of the name was Farnhurst (and variants) but in modern times it has firmly settled for Fernhurst. One peculiarity of the parish is that it originally included a strip of Hampshire, North Ambersham, within its boundaries. It has been conjectured that this might go back to the days when the men of Wessex invaded Sussex, and occupied this portion. Having failed to hold on to their conquered territory, they withdrew leaving behind families of settlers who continued to look upon themselves as Wessex folk. In 1913 the Ambershams were incorporated into the neighbouring parishes, and this little bit of Hampshire in Sussex was forced to change its allegiance.

No one can accuse the Fernhurst men of lack of versatility or resourcefulness. In 1903 a directory listed George Mills as Firewood Dealer and Income Tax Collector. A story from the 19th century tells of how a Fernhurst man got married and addressed the parson in this way 'I ain't got no money, y'know; y'must take it out in taties'. I hope present day Fernhurst men haven't changed too much.

Ferring

When the good people of Ferring hear a ghostly church bell, they know it to be the bell of Kingston chapel – which was swallowed up by the encroaching sea around 300 years ago. Now all that remains of the chapel are some stones which can be seen only when the tide is out.

The nearby Highdown Hill is visited by many curious people, not because of the Iron Age hill fort, or the Saxon burial ground, but because of the strange altar-like tomb of John Olliver – 'Miller Olliver', who dwelt in a mill on the hill. He was one of our famous Sussex eccentrics, making his own coffin years before he was likely to need it, and keeping it on castors under his bed. He also built his tomb 30 years before it was required. When he finally died at 84 in 1793, it was said that 2,000 people attended the funeral. The coffin was carried by bearers dressed all in white, and a young maiden read the sermon which he had chosen. Several legends surrrounded the burial of this unusual man; one is that he was buried upside down, so that on the day of judgement when the world is turned around, he would be right way up. Another is that the inscription on the tomb says that if one runs round it seven times (the magic number) the Devil will appear. Of course it says no such thing. One lady told me how when she was young she tried this with some of her friends, but no one had the courage to last out seven times. An epitaph, written by the miller himself, ran thus:

'Why should my fancy any one offend,
Whose good or ill does not on it depend;
'Tis at my own expense, except the land,
A generous grant on which my tomb doth stand;
This is the only spot that I have chose,
Wherein to take my lasting long repose;
Here in the dust my body lieth down,
You'll say it is not consecrated ground—
I grant the same, but where shall we e'er find,
The spot that e'er can purify the mind;
Nor to the body any lustre give,
This more depends on what a life we live;
For when the trumpet shall begin to sound,
T'will not avail e'en where the body's found!'

Even today John Olliver's tomb is still making the headlines, as in modern times vandals damaged it and the police were called in to investigate.

May Day was 'Garland Day' in Ferring, as elsewhere in Sussex in the late 19th century. The children of the village went around showing their pretty flower garlands, and asking for pennies, which were usually forthcoming as this was a custom most grownups enjoyed. One May Day in the 1880s young George Charles arrived at school 'noisy and almost intoxicated'. he had spent his Garland money on beer!

From the very young to the very old. In 1895 a Ferring couple died within a few days of each other, having lived as man and wife for almost 71 years.

Findon 🐑

Sheep Fairs on Findon's Nepcote Green go back to at least 1261, when a charter was granted by Henry III. Traditionally the fair was always held on September 14th, but in 1959 it was decided that the annual event should take place on the second Saturday of September. The dates of most Sussex fairs have some household or horticultural chore associated with them (Petworth fair day for planting broad beans, Crawley fair day for planting runner beans, and so on). Findon's original date of September 14th was always regarded as the day to start winter fires indoors.

The auctioneers, Churchman Burt and Son have been associated with the Findon Fair since 1896. Nowadays between 10,000 and 20,000 sheep are on offer, and business is normally very good. Every year the Sussex newspapers carry such headlines as 'Brisk Trade at Great Fair' or 'Business Brisk at Sheep Fair'. Originally there were two fairs a year, a lamb fair as well as the Great Fair of September 14th. The former was discontinued in 1971 due to a falling off of support. The Southdown Sheep Society Annual Show has been held in conjunction with the Findon Great Fair since 1951.

Many older folk remember the days when sheep were driven to the fair on their own four feet. As they came off the Downs with their shepherds dressed in finely worked smocks, they were described by one writer as looking like fluffy white clouds. The shepherds and drovers often started very early in the morning, or even on the day before, walking many miles with their flocks, and afterwards returning very late in the evening. When the railways came they took over the transportation of all but the nearer flocks, and sheep started to arrive at the fair from many other parts of the country – although they still had to be driven to Findon from Steyning railway station.

The number of sheep at the fair each year is seen as an indication of the health of sheep farming in Sussex. But not only sheep have been sold at the fair. There used to be cattle, horses with manes and tails plaited with coloured ribbons, donkeys and goats. There have always been amusement stalls and booths, and of course the gypsies with fortune telling and home-made sweets. The boxing booth was always a favourite with the local lads, particularly so in the year when Joe Beckett, who later became British Heavyweight Boxing Champion, challenged all comers to three rounds – those who lasted out gaining a silver crown for their fortitude.

Fair nights at the Gun Inn, were occasions to be remembered. It was said that more fights took place there than in the boxing booth at the fair. The culprits were usually shepherds who after a few beers loved to argue over the merits of their dogs, or their own shepherding skills.

Refreshment is also available at the fair itself, but there was a serious crisis a few years ago when the bar failed to arrive. The local hotel did their best to fill the gap, but could not provide all the liquid refreshment required by the thirsty shepherds. No doubt the Gun did particularly good business that year.

Country amusements still occupy a part of the fair grounds, and the tradition of a good day out is still very much to the fore.

An additional entertainment sometimes offered at the Gun, was a performer known as 'Titch' who fascinated his audience by juggling with bones, which he clapped together in rhythm.

A drink at the Gun may have been in the mind of a Findon firm when this advertisement was composed in the 19th century:

> 'The Necessaries of Life. A fire in Winter, a meal
> when hungry, a drink when thirsty, a bed at night,
> a friend in need, a Lucifer match in the dark, a
> good wife, a pipe of tobacco (if you like it), and
> your horses clipped well by Cooter and Son,
> Established 1841'.

Findon has a long history of connections with horses and horse racing. A blacksmith's shop was established in the village in 1760. At one time there were three forges in Findon, and a local riddle was to ask why all the blacksmiths were coloured men. The answer was that one smith was Mr Brown, another Mr White and the third Mr Green.

The church of St. John the Baptist which Nairn and Pevsner refer to as 'an odd lovable sight', in 1848 had a church band consisting of violin, bass viol, clarionet and flute. A pitch pipe was used to start the hymns, a big wooden affair, and sometimes when the plug got stuck a most discordant noise resulted. The bass viol in the band was played by the school master, and was purchased in 1798 for £3.13.6d.

The Liptrott Charity was established in Findon in 1887 to commemorate Queen Victoria's Jubilee. Miss Liptrott gave £150 to be invested; the interest to be used to purchase coal for six deserving villagers. In 1968 it was decided that groceries would be more useful than coal, but the interest that year was only £7.3.4d., hardly enough to buy groceries for even one person. But local organisations rallied round, and additional contributions enabled the trustees of the charity to provide 35 food parcels.

One of our Sussex eccentrics and one of the most interesting characters in Findon's past, was William Frankland who lived at Muntham Court in the 18th century. After a very adventurous life, he settled down in Findon for his last forty years, to study mechanical science. He invented many weird and wonderful machines, and his house was a veritable treasure store of large and small mechanical contraptions. He had a marvellous collection of clocks and watches, a whole room devoted to musical instruments, and another given over to printing machines. He kept many workers in employment, some of them from other countries. He is said to have spent £20,000 on his collection – a vast sum at that time. William Frankland died in 1805 aged 85 and his collection was sold for a large amount, one lathe alone fetching three thousand guineas.

The modern part of Findon is known as Findon Valley, but it is nice to see that the older village still manages to retain its original identity as an extremely lively and interesting place.

Fittleworth ✀

Arthur Beckett, that great champion of all things Sussex, called Fittleworth 'as sweet and pleasant a village as you shall find in Sussex'. I wouldn't disagree with him, and neither I fancy would the many artists, anglers and others who have visited, lingered and often stayed there through the years. Fittleworth's inn, the Swan, was celebrated by E.V. Lucas in this fashion: 'Probably the most ingeniously placed inn in the world.

Approaching it from the north it seems to be the end of all things: the miles of road that one has travelled apparently have been leading nowhere but to the Swan......Coming from the south, one finds that the road narrows by this inn almost to a lane, and the Swan's hospitable sign, barring the way, exerts such a spell that to enter is a far simpler matter than to pass'.

The Swan, Fittleworth
early this century

The Swan seems to have succeeded in being all things to all men. It was popular with visitors, and at the same time viewed with considerable affection by the locals. Linley Sambourne of *Punch* drew a picture of a snail in 1892, and wrote underneath it:

'If seeing this and reason fail,
And wonder says, 'Why draw a snail'?
The wherefore is, as snails are slow,
So the Swan's guests are loth to go'.

Another poet, this time anonymous, wrote in praise of the Swan's beverage:

'Who loves a glass of English ale,
Can get it at the Swan,
The flavour rich and colour bright,
The draught both old and strong'.

86

Although the Horsham-Pulborough railway line was opened in 1858, Fittleworth did not have a station until the 1880s. This helped the village to be discovered by artists, and many of them stayed at the Swan. They painted the mill, and the three bridges, and even on the panels within the inn itself.

Now Fittleworth station is no more, and it is difficult to believe that at one time there were 18 trains stopping there each day. It was an important station for the milk from local farms to be dispersed in those attractive yet functional upright milk churns, which were such a feature of country stations during the early years of this century. About 1,000 gallons of milk a day left via this little station, during the years up to about 1926.

On special occasions the blacksmiths at Fittleworth 'fired the anvil', loading it with powder and touching if off with a fuse to produce a noise like a cannon. It has been stated that at the time of the Spanish Armada, a warning of its approach was sounded by the Fittleworth smith in this manner.

Of course all good villages had a treasure and a witch. The buried treasure at Fittleworth is supposed to be in a wood, the clue being that the spot where the treasure is buried sounds hollow to the tread. A spirit guards the treasure from a nearby ditch, and appears if anyone approaches. One woman claimed to have seen the guardian and said it was dressed in brown. Naturally enough the villagers avoided the place after dark.

The witch lived in the village early in this century, and was ostracised by the residents, all except one lady, who was more enlightened (some would say foolhardy) than the rest, and went out of her way to talk to the old lady.

Mrs Latham of Fittleworth recalled how an old woman of the village claimed to be a dealer in charms. She assured Mrs Latham that many people came to her with bad wounds and got her to 'say her blessing over them'. This consisted of the following four lines recited:

> 'Our Saviour Christ was of a pure virgin born,
> And he was crowned with a thorn;
> I hope it may not rage nor swell;
> I trust in God it may do well'.

The wise-woman readily admitted that she had inherited

from her mother a charm for the bite of a viper, and another to cure giddiness in cattle. To her credit she never made any charge for her services.

Several years ago I visited Fittleworth fairly regularly to talk to an old friend, George Attrill, who lived in a cottage by himself – except for several cats – down a Sussex lane. He was a retired road mender, as was one of this brothers. Another worked in the stone quarries, and the fourth who had fits stayed at home and kept house for the others. Later Ben ended his days in Horsham workhouse, and when he died someone asked George if he would go to his brother's funeral. 'I don't think I will' was the reply. 'After all, he won't be coming to mine'.

George's recollections included old time sing-songs at the Swan, where he learnt many songs. He remembered when a ballad singer visited Fittleworth every few weeks, standing outside the Swan and offering his stock of ballad sheets at one penny and twopence each, advertising each one by singing it. Some of the old songs he said were so long, you needed three people to sing them. One to start at the beginning, one at the end and one in the middle. He recalled 'Rounds' being sung in the local pubs, and when one of the singers missed his part, he had to empty his glass. One of his songs ended up with this evocation of his favourite beverage:

> 'Then shout for great John Barleycorn, for heed his luscious vine,
> I have no mind much charm to find in potent draught of wine,
> Give me my native nut-brown ale, all other drinks I scorn,
> For true English cheer is English beer, our own John Barleycorn'.

George played Father Christmas in the 1930s revival of the traditional tipteering play. The rest of the cast included Billy Twing Twang, King George, Turkish Knight, Valiant Soldier, Doctor, and Prince of Peace. The words of the play were remembered by George who had acted in it as a boy. It was revived for a second time in 1945, with George again taking the part of Father Christmas, for which he needed no false beard.

The BBC invited the players to come to London for their play to be recorded but Father Christmas refused to leave his village. When George wrote to me to tell me about the play, he ended the letter with the words 'I should like to have been behind the scenes when you opened the letter, and took a snap of your face'. Typically he was gaining great pleasure just from giving me something which he knew I would enjoy and treasure. This wonderful old Sussex gentleman died in 1964 aged 78. I am grateful that I knew him.

I started this piece on Fittleworth with a quotation extolling the attractiveness of the village, so it seems appropriate to end with these lines from a poem by Arthur St. George, written in 1928:

> 'The leafy inn, the mellowed church,
> The kindly village folk,
> Reflect the glow of beauty's lucent blush.
> The singing mill, the nestling cottages,
> Acknowledge with enchanting evidence,
> Her soft caress'.

Flansham 🐚

Almost certainly most people will know little about this tiny village, unless they actually live there, or have read the books writen by Gerard Young in the 1940s. Mr Young wrote his first book, *The Chronicle of a Country Cottage,* in 1942, and I suspect that it was intended to be a 'one off' about his own weekend cottage and garden; which happened to be in the village of Flansham, which is close to Felpham, which is near Bognor Regis.

Flansham is of course quite small, without even a church, pub or shop, but few villages can have had such a conscientious historian and observer. Gerard Young worked all the week in a job connected with the theatre, often travelling all over the country, but at weekends he returned whenever he could to his cottage in the village where he found most happiness and peace. In *Come into the Country* (1945) he describes Flansham in this fashion:

'Like most villages, no one has ever heard of it and no one can ever find it. Even if I tell you the name of it, which is Flansham, it will convey nothing to you. It is a dead-end village; two lanes which lead to nowhere, a village which succesfully frustrates the summer evening motorists who rattle up the lane with a condescending smile for the men still working in the meadows, and few minutes later rattle back again without a condescending smile, having landed up in a ploughed field'.

Not much to write about in such a place, one would think, but Gerard Young wrote with a light but affectionate touch, letting us into the innermost secrets of the village and particularly of the people who lived in the handful of farmhouses and cottages. We hear about the Adames family who farmed with tremendous enthusiasm, the Page family, Mrs Jacks, and Jack Langmead, another farmer. They all come alive in the pages of these books, and we slowly realise what an exciting place little Flansham really is.

One of Gerard Young's delights was to talk about Cuthbert, the family ghost at Flansham Manor. He made it plain that there was nothing sinister about this ghost, in fact it always gave every evidence of being extremely friendly. Cuthbert was a little shy, and always vanished rather apologetically whenever anyone came upon him in one of the passages of the Manor. Many people saw him however, and most were in agreement that he wore grey flannel trousers. Guests were sometimes a little wary of Cuthbert and it took a time for them to accept him quite as easily as did the regulars. Cuthbert was apparently Flansham's only ghost, and there seemed to be no explanation for his appearances or indeed for his predilection for grey flannel trousers.

In spite of its unimportance, Flansham was the home for many years of a man who produced some very beautiful books, all of which are now collector's items. The Pear Tree Press was run by James Guthrie from his house in the village, from 1907 to 1952. The village knew little of him or of his lovely books, but connoisseurs of the craft of hand printing, all over the world, looked upon him as a master. He started his own press as long ago as 1899 at Ingrave in Essex, continuing at Shorne in Kent in 1900, then at Harting, and finally Flansham. In Festival of Britain year he wrote, designed, and printed the book *From a Sussex Village,* in a limited edition of 300 copies, selling it at the incredibly low price of ten shillings. The book was of course about Flansham and its residents. I may add that I have never seen a copy for sale, and if I do, I know I will have to pay many times the original price if I am to own it. On October 25th at the age of 78, James Guthrie died from a heart atack while out walking. To quote Gerard Young, he was 'a rare man with the cherubic face of a kindly bishop'. He was also something of a genius.

Ford 🦡

A village with a name which needs no explanation; in fact there were probably two fords here in days gone by. Many will know it either as the site of a now defunct aerodrome, or as an open prison, which in recent years has caused considerable controversy.

The tiny church of St. Andrew is described by Pevsner and Nairn as 'one of Sussex's prettiest churches; a lovable unrestored exterior..... humble village interior'. Earlier writers were less complimentary. Horsfield in 1835 commented 'The church is small and contains nothing of interest'. In 1904 E.V. Lucas said 'popular rumour has it that its minute and uninteresting church was found one day by accident in a bed of nettles

Certainly the church was neglected for several years, and at one time was roofless, which led to a local saying 'Ford church was lost among the stinging nettles'. When it was restored in 1865 the font was thrown out, and left in a farmyard as a bath for the ducks. Several jars were found built into the walls, whether as early acoustic aids or for some other reason is not clear.

A parish priest in 1535, John Forbe, left a will in which he promised 'tenpence to every mayden of marriageable age and fourpence to every mayd of ten years, if they came to his funeral'. An old Sussex bell rhyme prosaically offers 'Bread and cheese on a board, says the bells of Ford'.

91

The bellcote of the church is painted white; someone unkindly suggesting that this was to prevent it being lost again.

No one of great fame seems to have lived at Ford. The best I can find is Mr. William Garraway who resided there in the 17th century, and when he was 81 had such a wonderful memory he was described as a walking library. He fasted completely on one day each week, and was almost completely teetotal.

Fulking

At the beginning of the 19th century there were said to be 2,600 sheep in the parish of Fulking, with but only 258 humans. At this time, and for many years before, sheep and Fulking were synonymous, and the local hostelry, Shepherd and Dog was aptly named.

'The Shepherd and Dog' pub, Fulking

Many other downland villages sent their sheep to Fulking to be washed in May or June, before the annual sheep shearing. The spring of clear water which rises here was eminently suitable for the purpose, and a dam was made to hold the stream, whilst the sheep were kept in readiness in a pen. The washing was carried out by two or three men who stood in the cold water for several hours. The main road ran through the centre of operations, and during the time of the washing was closed to traffic, until a man opened a gate at each end to let a vehicle through. Of course there was little traffic in those days, with probably only two or three carts passing through the village in a day.

When the sheep washing came to an end for the day, the men involved would walk the short distance to the Shepherd and Dog, stiff with cold, and with water drippng from them. Rheumatism took its toll of these heroes, and normally they could only continue this job for a few years.

Following the sheep washing, came the annual shearing. This was carried out by an expert gang of men, who met to plan their itinerary at the home of the captain. This meeting was known as 'The White Ram', and would be followed by a meal. A lieutenant assisted the captain, and they both wore special hats, carrying gold and silver braid. An important member of the team was the tar boy, whose job it was to apply tar to any cuts on the sheep, to prevent infection. Too many shouts for the tar boy meant that the shearer was not particularly expert.

The men were expected to shear 30 to 40 sheep in a day, and the farmer was called upon to supply them with a midday meal and beer while they worked. At the end of each day, the gang expected to be provided with another meal and more beer. The evenings were spent in drinking, smoking long clay pipes and singing.

The master was the farmer employing them, and was the usual term used by agricultural workers for their boss, in those less complicated days.

At the completion of the sheep shearing the whole company would meet again for a meal at the Shepherd and Dog, and the earnings were shared out, and arrangements made for next year. This meeting was called 'The Black Ram', and the song *The Rose-buds in June* was invariably featured.

> 'Here the rose-buds in June, and the violets are blowing;
> The small birds they warble, from every green bough;

> Here's the pink and the lily, and the
> daffydowndilly,
> To adorn and perfume the sweet meadows in
> June.
> 'Tis all before the plough the fat oxen go slow;
> But the lads and the lasses to the sheep-shearing
> go.'

The members of the company then dispersed to their normal occupations, until it was time for another sheep shearing.

The Shepherd and Dog which was once so popular with the shepherds and the shearing gangs, still provides shepherd's lunches, ploughman's lunches, fisherman's lunches and several other varieties, but the customers are mainly motorists who come from a wide area around, such is the fame of the fare provided. On a typical Sunday the small car park is crowded, and the customers' cars spill out onto the road on both sides of the very sharp bend by the inn.

Just around the corner, and close to where the sheep washing used to be carried out, is the village fountain. The brickwork surround was erected by a local brewer to commemorate John Ruskin, who helped the village with its water supply. The following appears on one wall, done in Victorian letter tiles:

> 'He sendeth springs into the valley which run
> among the hills
> Oh that men would praise the Lord for his
> goodness.'

One minor curiosity is that several of the 'S's are upside down. When Arthur Beckett, the Sussex author, asked a villager for information on the fountain, he was told that it was put up to 'Sir John Ruskin, by a gent as uster live here. Very good water, Sir, it come from the 'ills, and don't see the light till it come from that 'ere spout'. Unfortunately Ruskin was not a 'Sir', and as to the purity of the water, I can only report that there is now a sign which says 'Not fit for drinking'.

Funtington 🌿

The name of this neat little village was formerly pronounced
'Funnington' by its natives. A local chapel was said to have been
built with stones which once formed the spire of Chichester
Cathedral. At its opening the text of the sermon was reported as
being 'the glory of the latter house shall be greater than the
former.'

Horsfield, who was not normally given to extravagant praise,
says in his *History, Antiquities and Topography of the County
of Sussex* (1835) 'The Salubrity of the air is so remarkable, that
this district may be justly styled the Montpelier of England.'

Goring 🌿

The great natural history writer, Richard Jefferies, lived the
final years of his life at Jefferies House, Goring. He died there
in 1887 and is buried in Broadwater cemetery. His writings
contain many references to Sussex, although the places
described are not always identifiable.

The choir in the church once consisted of schoolgirls,
wearing white straw poke bonnets trimmed with white cambric,
and pink and white print dresses and capes. They must have
looked very fetching.

In the 17th century the village was visited by a traveller, John
Taylor. He later published a poem on his tour, which was not
very complimentary to Goring. It begins:

> 'A town called Goreing stood neere two miles
> wide,
> To which we went and had our wants supplide:
> There we relieved ourselves (with good
> compassion),
> With meat and lodging of the homely fashion.
> To bed we went in home of rest and ease,
> But all beleaguered with an host of fleas:
> Who in theiry fury nip't and skip't so hotly,
> That all our skins were almost turned to motley.

When we (opprest with their increasing pow'rs),
Were glad to yeeld the honour of the day,
Unto our foes and rise and runne away'.

But remember that was in 1623!

The *Sussex County Magazine* of September 1927 carried an
account of life in Goring in 1840-52, which was much more
pleasant. Its reminiscences came from a lady of 92, a few years
before she died. She remembered Squire Stanhope driving
about the village with his silver hair black-ribboned; surely the
last wearer of the pig-tail! The main diversions were hay-
making jollifications and Harvest Homes. At hay-making the
men sang:

> 'Jug, jug, sweet, sweet, the nightingale doth sing,
> From the morning until evening as we are hay-
> making.
> Our wives and sweethearts we regale,
> With home-spun jest and nut-brown ale –
> Laddie-tum-day, Laddie-tum-day,
> We'll all go make the new-mown hay!'

After harvesting they stood in a ring in the stack-yard and
shouted:

> 'We've ploughed, we've sowed, we've reaped,
> we've mowed,
> We've carried our last harvest load!
> Hip, hip, hip hooray!
> Send out the maids with ribands flying –
> Good mistress with the steddle-cup,
> For we with drouth comes near a-dying,
> And we has set our last sheaf up.
> Hip, hip, hip hooray!'

At Christmas time she recalled the 'wastlers' (wassailers)
arriving with a great shuffling of heavy feet and singing:

> 'Good Master and good Mistress a-sitting
> by your fire –

96

Remember we poor Wastlers have trudged
through mud and mire:
Send out your eldest daughter, if you will be so
kind,
Send out your eldest daughter with strong beer
and some wine'.

A microcosm of Sussex social history in four short lines.

Graffham 🦐

A long winding uphill street, leading to a pretty church, where
Cardinal Manning was rector in the 19th century, before his
conversion to Roman Catholicism.

The Petworth Society bulletin provides a lovely story about
Grannie Pratt of Graffham, who used to lay out the dead of the
village. She also combined this with other duties, and when one
old lady said that her husband was unlikely to last the night,
Grannie Pratt replied 'I'll come round in the morning, but if he
isn't dead by 9 o'clock, I can't do it. I've got to be pig killing all
morning'.

There is an intriguing legend about Garton Orme, a local
landowner in Georgian times. According to tradition, Orme
was an ogre who starved and murdered his wife, in favour of a
village beauty. Opinion was firm among the villagers that he
disposed of his wife's body down a well; but Orme duly
produced a coffin and had it interred in the proper manner in
the family vault. A century later, alterations were being made to
the church, and the coffin came to light. The rector, surprised
by its weight, had it opened, to reveal a load of stones. As is so
often the case, a local tradition was based on fact. A ghost of a
pale female figure seen near the well, even in modern times,
adds further interest to the legend. Yet another strand in the
story connects a willow tree beside the well with the fortunes of
the Orme family.

Another Graffham story is about a highwayman – making a
change from the usual smugglers of Sussex tradition. His name
was Allen, and he worked the roads between Arundel and
Chichester, around 1807. After many successful robberies, the

militia were called out to capture him, and following a chase he took refuge near Graffham pond. After a skirmish, the robber was killed, but not before he had managed to despatch one of his pursuers with his pistol.

It is a far cry from ogres, ghosts and highwaymen to modern oil exploration, but in recent times crude oil has been found at Baxter's Copse, Graffham. Now the residents are divided over whether if the oil find proves to be commercially economic, it will be a good or a bad thing for the future of the village.

Halnaker ✿

Pronounced Hannaker, the name has puzzled people for a long, long time. The popular explanation is that it refers to a lack of cultivation on one side of the village, in other words half-naked, although this suggestion is now out of favour. At different times it has been spelled in different ways – Helnache, Halnac, Halfnakede and Holnaker.

The most interesting building is the brick tower mill which stands on Halnaker Hill. One of the oldest windmills in existence, with walls 4 feet thick, it was built about 1750 and restored in 1934 and again in 1955. It stands very four-square, compared to the elegance of some of the later more sophisticated mills.

The site seems to have been a popular place for mills; one is recorded there as early as c. 1540. The present mill ceased working in 1900, and in 1913 high winds carried the sails away. Later fresh sails were provided, and although the interior machinery has been removed, the mill once again looks complete.

During the Second World War the mill was used as an observation post and also as a navigational aid for aircraft. In 1958 the West Sussex County Council accepted responsibility for the mill, along with Salvington Post Mill and Shipley Smock Mill, thus ensuring that there would be one good example of each of the three main types of windmills preserved in the county. Hilaire Belloc used 'Ha'nacker Mill' as the title for one of his Sussex poems.

The original Halnaker House became a ruin about 1800, and

all that remain now are a few walls. There is a later Halnaker House, by Lutyens, built in 1938.

One of the county's many reminders of 'Old Nick' is a six mile ditch running from near Halnaker to near West Stoke. It is known simply as 'the Devil's Ditch', although as far as I know, and unlike other similar sites, it does not appear to have any particular Devil legend attached to it.

Handcross 🌿

E.V. Lucas called it 'a Clapham Junction of highways', but this was in 1904 before it was bypassed. More recently Ian Nairn and Nikolaus Pevsner referred to it as 'a cheerful village'. It has always seemed to me to be a bustling sort of place, and indeed the residents must have felt they were being rushed into the 20th century a bit too quickly when in 1906 the London to Brighton motor bus crashed here, causing the death of 10 people and injuring 24 more. Accidents of this sort were not commonplace at this time, and the disaster seems to have caused a good deal of excitement and consternation. Picture postcards of the accident were quickly made available, and must have found a ready sale as they still turn up not infrequently.

In the previous century walking must have been the principle form of locomotion for the majority, and in 1880 a Mr. Hart of Lindfield and Mr. Hobden of Haywards Heath agreed on a 5 mile walking race starting from Handcross. Mr. Hart won by 200 yards, but lost his bet based on the time he expected to take.

A craft more usually associated with East Sussex, that of trug-basket making, was formerly carried on in the neighbourhood, and this is commemorated by the name of a housing estate – 'Truggers'.

Handcross School celebrated its centenary in 1978, with the publication of a 120 page book by the Parent Aid Committee. The original buildings cost £1,636 in 1878, although their completion was delayed by of all things, a strike among the workmen. The first master was paid £150 per annum, and the school cleaner earned six shillings a month. Among the latter's duties was the lighting of the school fires daily; the boiler requiring twelve scuttles of coal to get it going.

At about the same time Handcross also had a Dame's School kept by a Mrs Wenham. She seems to have been a slightly frightening old lady who punished her pupils by making them wear a dunce's cap, and sitting them in the doorway where all could see them as they passed by.

In the late 19th century May Day was considered very important, and each child would bring a garland of flowers to school, and then march to the church for a special service. Afterwards they visited the big houses with their garlands and were suitably rewarded with coins and refreshments.

This charming book continues with much more similar social history through the years right up to the time of publication, and the compilers are to be congratulated on a splendid compilation of local material.

Hardham ᘉ

Once an important Roman posting station on Stane Street, but now an inconspicuous hamlet close to the Arun. The main road is a bypass, leaving Hardham but a short distance away separated from the hurrying coastbound traffic by green grass and hedges.

Hardham's particular glory lies in the simple church of St. Botolph. Built in the 11th century it possesses what is possibly the most complete set of early wall paintings in any church in the British Isles. The murals were executed about 1120-40, supposedly on the instigation of the Priory of St. Pancras at Lewes. They were covered in the 13th century and remained hidden until the mid 19th century. In 1862 the hidden works of art were hinted at when someone decided to chip off some of the plaster to show the bare stone. At this point one of the paintings was virtually destroyed, but in 1866 the rest of the murals were disclosed more-or-less intact.

They are in two tiers, and were probably copies by unknown artists from early manuscripts. The pictures include representations of nativity scenes, the torments of the souls in Hell, St. George, the Annunciation and the Visitation. Because of their age, the time they were covered, and possibly the way they were uncovered, the paintings give only a vague idea of what a typical 11th century English church must have been like; but with a little imagination one can obtain some idea of the way our Christian ancestors learnt the scripture stories and how they worshipped at mass in what must have been a riot of colour.

Hardham Church had its anchorite in his cell built against the wall of the church. The cell has of course disappeared, but the squint cut in the stonework remains. This gave him a view of the high altar and enabled him to receive the sacred host.

Close to the Arun water meadows are the remains of Hardham Priory, now incorporated into a farmhouse. A fire in 1912 exposed some 14th century wall paintings, but we can only guess at what else is hidden, as the site has not been excavated.

Hardham has a tunnel on the canal, too narrow for barges to pass through by any other means but with the bargeman lying on his back and 'treddling' the craft along the roof. Woe betide the unfortunate who got his barge wedged halfway along the tunnel.

There were stories concerned with smugglers, and also connecting the tunnel in some way with Hardham Priory, but these seem to be very unsubstantial.

There was a mill at Hardham, until a stray bomb hit it in the Second World War. Mr. Frank Strickland, who emigrated to Kansas in 1912, recalled some unpleasant memories of the mill in an American milling journal in 1964. One of these concerns the rat's tails for which the mill workers were paid one penny. Each tail represented a dead rat, and the tails were kept for an indefinite time in the mill office. As may be expected, the place stank of them.

Harting

There are actually three Hartings: South, West and East; although it is the village of South Harting that mainly concerns us. W.H. Hudson, who was much travelled and whose opinions must therefore carry some weight, said 'The village of South Harting itself is not unworthy of its setting of green hills and purple woods. Of all the downland villages it is to my mind the most attractive. It is moreover, distinct and individual, without any resemblance to the others...' He went on to say that although the church at Alfriston has been called 'The Cathedral of the Downs', for pure beauty it cannot compare with that of South Harting.

The church dedicated to St Mary and St Gabriel is big, with much of interest, including the war memorial by Eric Gill. Outside are the remains of the village stocks, and a whipping post with iron straps for wrists belonging to criminals of different heights. The stocks were last used in earnest about 1860, although they were later used in a lighthearted manner around 1870.

Harvest suppers were normally fairly innocent affairs, but at South Harting they expected some heavy drinking. Here it was the custom of the farmer to lay down a quantity of straw outside the barn, so that the revellers, when they became 'consarned in liquor' could be taken out by their mates and laid on the ground until such time as they had recovered sufficiently to return and resume drinking. In 1881 the Salvation Army was active in Harting, and a group in the village who objected to their style of religion, raised their own band of 'rough music' to provide opposition to the army's brass.

But the best parade in South Harting has always been on Whit Monday, when the Harting Old Club holds its annual Club Day. The benefit club was founded in either 1800 or 1812 (probably the former), and is still going strong. In 1981, although the membership was a little down, the annual feast was still taking place, and the traditions and objectives still continue. The three main events on Club Day are the walk through the village, the church service and the feast. A history of the club by M.R. Perham was published in 1958.

Harting's treasure legend is connected with Tarberry hill, to the north of the village. Folklore says that the hill was formed from a spoon which the Devil had been using to sup hot punch from his Punch Bowl in Surrey. A treasure left behind by the Royalists is supposed to be buried here. The rhyme runs:

'Who'd know what Tarberry would bear,
Must plough it with a golden share.'

The nature of the treasure is not specified.

Harting has several connections with literature. John Caryll lived here and Gilbert White owned several properties around the area. However, the most important literary figure connected with the village was Anthony Trollope, who came from London in 1880, and lived here until shortly before his death in 1882. In this short time he wrote four novels, working as always to a system of 250 words every fifteen minutes, until he had reached 2,500 words – and all this before breakfast. This conveyor-belt attitude to writing enabled him to make £70,000 from his pen during his lifetime. He said 'We go to church and mean to be good', and as he had taken a lease of 17 years on his property, he evidently intended to stay and become a country gentleman.

The last time I visited South Harting was on a glorious summer's day, with the village holding its annual fete. The lovely village street was closed to traffic, covered with stalls and bunting, and the church decorated with flowers. There was even a craft fair in one of the inn yards, and along came the village band playing *Sussex by the Sea*. It was almost too good to be true, and if I had wanted to show a visitor a little bit of traditional Sussex, this is just what I would have wished for.

Heyshott

Heyshott, near Midhurst, has the distinction of once having had a house which was half in Sussex and half in Hampshire. Fortunately a revision of the boundaries in the 18th century placed the whole building firmly in Sussex.

The village's most famous resident was the great free-trader and reformer Richard Cobden. He was born there on 3rd June 1804, his father being a small farmer. In 1828 he was able to establish his own business, leasing a factory in Lancashire to print calicoes. The business thrived and he was able to devote much of his time to public work. He became passionately devoted to the cause of free-trade, and in 1837 made his first attempt to enter Parliament, standing for Stockport, but polling only 418 votes. Undeterred he played a forceful part in the formation of the anti-corn law league, and in 1841 won Stockport at the General Election. He continued to fight with every means at his disposal for the repeal of the corn duty, but it

103

was not until 1849 that his cause finally won the day. Cobden had wrecked his health and ruined himself financially in the struggle, and a subscription was opened to help him with his debts and to buy a small property at Heyshott where he could live and recover his health. He continued to be very energetic in public duties until he died in London on 2nd April 1865, being buried in the Sussex he loved at Lavington churchyard.

During his life he moved among the most exalted and powerful, but he liked to mix with the ordinary Sussex folk, even sharing their humble meals when he had the opportunity. Some idea of how he was viewed in his own village can be gauged by this account by Thomas Wrapson, wood-sawyer of Heyshott, printed in a penny pamphlet about 1900.

'What we mostly cared about wor to keep off the parish. But things changed, I can tell'ee, when Mr. Cobden come I wor a-workin' then at Box mill, for tenpence a day, an' Mr. Frederick Cobden, who'd often be passin' 'ud say 'Well, young Wrapson, why don't ee get somethin' better to do?' an' I didn't know what to answer; an' then Mr. Cobden 'e took me on an' paid me two shillun' a day 'e did. Wages was riz all round; them that used to work for 7s. a week, Mr. Cobden he give 12s. an' 15s. a week to, an' o'course the farmers 'as to riz their wages too, or they'd 'a found themselves wi'out any men......I often saw Mr. Cobden about, an' sometimes 'e'd speak to me, but more often than not 'e'd be sunk that deep in studdy that 'e never noticed nobody; 'e seemed allus a-plannin' something'.

And perhaps as an epitaph, none could be better than this from George Pollard, labourer of Heyshott.

'Folks was rare sorry when Mr. Cobden died; 'e did a power for Heyshott; 'e did; 'e wor the best man what ever come here'.

Horsted Keynes ✍

Horsted Keynes (for Caines, as it is pronounced) is a distinctly interesting village; for instance it features in the following tale concerning the introduction of potatoes into Sussex. William Warnett of Horsted Keynes, when aged over 90, said that before 1765 when he was seven years old, potatoes had never been heard of in his neighbourhood; in that year Lord Sheffield, who had recently purchased the Sheffield Estate, brought some over from Ireland, and his father received some from his lordship's gardener. No one knew how they should be planted, but a roadman who came from another county planted them, and continued to do so each year on old Lady Day. It was a long time before anyone planted them in the fields. They used to leave the potatoes in the ground all the winter, covering them with brakes, and digging them up as they were wanted. Before potatoes came into use, Pease Pudding was the most popular vegetable, and even after the former were being grown, there was great prejudice against them. At a Lewes election 'No Popery, No Potatoes' was a popular cry.

In the pretty church of St. Giles there is an effigy of a little Crusader Knight, only 27 inches long, including a lion at the feet. The knight is crossed legged; the hands having been broken off, but they may have held a heart. In fact this was probably a 'Heart Shrine', with the crusader's heart buried beneath it, and the actual body left in a foreign land, a not unusual practice.

The church clock played tunes every three hours, early in the present century, and boys from other villages would walk miles to hear it. The tune sequence started with *Rule Britannia*, then *Abide With Me, Home Sweet Home,* and *Robin Adair*. The clock took ten minutes to wind, at regular intervals.

There was a 'Holy Well' on the Lindfield Road. The surroundings were boggy, so it was not easy to get to the chalybeate spring, but the practice was to throw a bottle on a long string several times, until enough liquid had been collected. It was used mainly for bathing the eyes, but not only humans benefited as dogs were thrown in to cure them of mange. This was the time of natural remedies; another one practised at Horsted Keynes was to make Toast Water (or

105

Donkey Tea as it was sometimes called) – one poured boiling water on to toasted home-made bread, and this was then stained, and when cool, drunk by those feeling sick or feverish. It was also given to children as a night-time drink, but as one lady told me, she would have preferred plain water.

Sussex was not noted for Plough Monday ceremonies, but a farm at Horsted Keynes had its own particular custom connected with the start of the ploughing season in January. It was known as 'winning the cock' and was described in the *Sussex County Magazine* in 1927 by a correspondent who remembered it from his childhood. The carter's boy brought his whip into the farm kitchen, whipping the table and counting up to nine as he did so. If he could get through this three times and get out of the house without water being thrown over him, he had 'won the cock'. In the unlikely event of the boy being successful, he was presented with the, for then, lordly sum of three and sixpence.

In 1883 the population of the parish had risen to 1,149 (from 777 in 1831). By 1901 it was down to 888. The strange increase was due to the building of the railway, with many navvies included in the census. The railway station was built about a mile from the village, and was therefore not used as much as it might have been. Many people visit it today, when travelling on the famous 'Bluebell Line' preserved railway, which runs from Sheffield Park, five miles away. It is a stout climb most of the way, crossing the river Ouse and then wandering through woods and fields in the heart of the beautiful Sussex weald.

Most of the staff of the line are volunteers, many of them giving up all their weekends to fill the various functions involved in running a railway. The headquarters of the line is at Sheffield Park, and I recall soon after the line opened being ticked off very thoroughly by the station master for walking across the tracks. (The volunteer staff take their job very seriously, as they should, where the public's safety is concerned). After an apology, friendly relations were resumed. There is plenty to interest railway enthusiasts; apart from the wonderful collection of steam locomatives and period rolling stock, there is a museum of railway relics, and even the old advertising plates on the station are worth looking at. The

The Bluebell Line, Horsted Keynes

Bluebell Line is a definite must for any visitors to this part of Sussex.

In the 17th century, we find another Sussex character, the Rev. Giles Moore, rector of Horsted Keynes, who left us his journals for the years 1656-1679.

Giles Moore was a typical clergyman of his time. He never travelled far from Sussex, and although a Royalist at heart, he compounded with Oliver Cromwell and in 1655 became rector of the village, remaining there until his death 24 years later. He ruled his parishioners sternly, quarrelling with the well-off ones over their tythes, but marrying and burying the poorer ones without charge – and often giving them gifts when he felt they were in need. Apart from occasional trips to London, he farmed, and raised game cocks for cock-fighting each Shrove Tuesday. He seems to have been a blunt sort of fellow, with a quick temper, but extremely generous, and probably highly esteemed by most of his flock.

His diaries are full of quotable items, so I must content myself with just a few at random.

'This being King Charles II coronation, I gave my
namesake Moore's daughter then married ten
shillings and the fiddlers sixpence.'
'I gave my wyfe a barrel of oysters and pottle of
claret, which, together with the carriage came to
six shillings and sixpence.'
'I arrested Thomas Chamberlayne whom the
same night I kept at Hd. Caines Parsonage, and
carried the next day to Lindfield, where in the
night hee made his escape from William
Batchelors, from both the bailiffs then tending
him, who it is supposed were bribed to connive at
it....'
'Ann Sayers of Lindfield came to live with mee as
mayd servant, with whom I bargained not, for
under forty shillings a yeare shee sayde shee would
not serve. I gave her sixpence.'
'I gave the Howling Boys sixpence.'

The last entry is the one most often mentioned, when the
subject of wassailing the apple trees in Sussex comes up. The
wassailing was usually done by a group of men or boys on New
Year's Eve or the eve of the Epiphany, although Giles Moore's
entry was on 26th December, so the Howling Boys, which was
the Sussex name for wassailers, must have been early that year.

The Horsted Keynes diarist died in 1679 and his diary came
to an end after this entry for the 3rd August:

'I prayed to captain Fishenden for a cephalic
playster and to Mr. Marshall, of Lewes, for a
Julep, and for something to make mee sleep, two
shillings and sixpence.'

In 1939 the then rector of Horsted Keynes, F. Stenton
Earley, had his history of the church and parish published, and
one of his chapters is devoted to the Rev. Giles Moore. The
Sussex Record Society also published an edited edition of the
Journal, in 1971.

Houghton

No Sussex story seems to have caught the popular imagination quite so thoroughly as the flight and escape of the future Charles II. Many Sussex villages have legends and tales connected with King Charles, but Houghton's is more substantial than many. After a narrow squeak in Houghton Forest, Charles and his party stopped for refreshment at the George and Dragon. Lawrence P. Burgess tells the story in a poem printed in the *Sussex County Magazine* in 1952:

'Upon a tranquil August day,
In sixteen-fifty-one,
A weary horseman halted there,
Ate, drank, and then was gone.

As down the road towards the bridge,
The horses hooves did ring,
None present guessed this man to be,
A hunted, harrassed king.'

The lovely Houghton Bridge has fascinated artists thoughout its long history, in fact the whole area hereabouts is painter's country, and these have included John Constable and Arthur Rackham. Not only were artists attracted by the tranquil countryside, but recluses also. At Houghton there once lived a hermitress of such holiness that she attracted the attention of St. Richard of Chichester, who is said to have bestowed a much needed bequest on her.

Although the village is really only one street, Nairn and Pevsner *(The Buildings of England, Sussex.* 1965) who do not bestow their praise lightly, comment that the church of St. Nicholas, although rebuilt in 1857, has more character and common sense than most c.19 restorations.

Hurstpierpoint

Often shortened to 'Hurst' by those who live hereabouts, the rather awkward sounding complete name is derived from a

Wooded Hill, and the family of De Peirpoint, who originated in Normandy and owned land here after the Norman conquest up until 1431.

The large church of Holy Trinity was built in 1843-5 on the site of what Nairn and Pevsner call 'a sweet villagey one'. A mile away is St. John's College which enjoys an excellent reputation in Sussex. Built in 1851-3 it is one of the three Canon Woodard schools in the county – the others being Lancing and Ardingly.

In Hurstpierpoint lived a schoolmistress Elizabeth Hitchener who, after corresponding with Shelley, joined his household for a short time. When she left, it was with a promise of £100 a year, to compensate for the loss of her school.

The Rev. Sabine Baring-Gould, best known as a West Country clergyman-writer, spent some time as a schoolmaster at Hurstpierpoint. While in Sussex he published a small collection of *Noels and Carols of French Flanders*.

Hurst is also one of the several places in Sussex with its own diarist. Thomas Marchant lived at Little Park, and kept a journal from 1714. There is much on old customs and social history. For instance on January 14th 1718 he wrote: 'A mountebank came to our towne today. He calls himself Dr. Richard Harness. Mr. Scutt and I drank tea with the tumbler. Of his tricks I am no judge; but he appears to me to play well on the fiddle'. And on September 19th 1719: 'John Parsons began his year last Tuesday. He is to shave my face twice a week, and my head once a fortnight, and I am to give him 100 faggots per annum'. Squire Marchant was buried on September 17th 1728, and his diary came to an end.

The village has much folklore. An old rhyme goes:

> 'When Wolsonbury has a cap,
> Hurstpierpoint will get a drap'.

In other words when a certain point of the Downs is covered by cloud, rain will follow at Hurstpierpoint.

Hurst was one of the places in Sussex where St. Crispin's Day (25th October) was once kept rather like November 5th in other villages. Bonfires were lit and the local lads went round the houses begging for pennies.

Jacqueline Simpson in *The Folklore of Sussex* (1973) tells

some fascinating stories about Nanny Smart, a witch who lived in the late 18th century. She was much feared for her ability to put people into a trance; and more commonly in a witch, to immobilise horses. It was also said that she could enter anyone's house and be given tea, as no one wished to annoy her by refusing. The best story of all concerns the belief that she could not die until someone bought the secrets of her life. Finally a Cuckfield man, Old Hockland, bought them from her for a halfpenny, and 'she died in a blue flame'. The man who bought her secrets died in Hurstpierpoint workhouse in the 1830s.

More recent Hurstpierpoint history brings us up to 1925, when the old knife-board bus 'Ye Olde Times' finally ceased to operate between Hurst and Hassocks. The following year it was a great attraction at the Lord Mayor's Show in London. The driver, who worked in the open whatever the weather, wore a rabbit-skin under his jacket to keep him warm during the winter. Inside, metal footwarmers filled with hot water were provided for the passengers.

Ifield 🌿

Once a compact village in its own right, Ifield is now part of Crawley New Town. But unlike other units of Crawley, it has its own village green, a church (St. Margaret), a Quaker meeting house, and a mill pond with mill.

The meeting house is in fact a cottage, built in 1676. The Minutes of the Monthly Meeting of February 1675 stated:

> 'That Arthur Standbridge ye Elder and William
> Garton and Richard Dunton and Arthur
> Standridge the younger did take care to see that
> Meeting House at Ifield builded according as it is
> agreed on.
> It is agreed that the said meeting house be builded
> with stone walls the length thereof not exceeding
> forty feet and the breadth not exceeding twenty
> four feet'.

It is thought that the stone for the walls came from Slaugham

111

Place. The roof is of Horsham stone, and the building is supported by a heavy oak pillar rising from floor to ceiling, which an expert stated was once a growing tree which the builders had shaped and used where it stood. The total cost was about £250.

In the churchyard of St. Margarets, a famous editor of *Punch,* Mark Lemon, lies in a simple grave. Born in London, he founded first *The Field,* and then with help from others, *Punch;* being its first editor at a wage of thirty shillings a week.

A lady who actually lives at Ifield, surprised me at the end of one of my talks, by asking me where was Ifield Mill. Ironically, although I do not live there, I see it every day on my way to London by train. The pond was man-made during the 16th century. It is now bisected by the main Victoria-Bognor railway line. Originally a hammer pond during the Sussex Iron Age, it later became a mill pond. The mill building started its life as an iron forge in the 16th century, was rebuilt in the 17th century as a corn mill, and was out of use from 1927 until 1974 when it was acquired by the Crawley Borough Council. In that year an agreement was reached with the council for a group of volunteers to begin the daunting task of restoring and rebuilding, so that eventually it can become a local museum.

The water mill had competition from 1837 when a windmill was built on the common. This continued in use, with steam helping out when wind power was not available, until early in the 20th century.

A thoughtful survey of Ifield Mill and the area immediately around it, was written by J. Gibson-Hill and E.W. Henbery, and published in 1979.

Lastly, a local recipe, Ifield Vicarage Hog's Pudding, contributed by Evelyn Manvel:

> 1 lb Pork
> 1 lb Currants
> A little baking powder
> Some sausage skins
> 1½ lbs flour
> 1 lb lard
> A little allspice

Cut the meat into small pieces and put on to boil gently for about 1 hour. Mix the flour with the meat, currants and spice and rub in the lard. Fill sausage skins and tie up in bunches. Prick the sausages with a fork and drop into boiling water. Boil them for 1½ hours. Take out and hang up to dry. They will snap when broken in two. Hog's Pudding is usually the size of an egg and irregular in shape and is usually eaten as a savoury either hot or cold.

Itchingfield 🦃

A small village, which has somehow been overlooked by many books on Sussex, although it has several interesting old buildings, including the delightful Priest's House in the churchyard, which one author described as looking like 'a toy'. It was here that in pre-Reformation times, travelling priests from Sele Priory, collecting tithes, would rest and take refreshment before saying mass in the church and moving on. The oldest part is 15th century, and the rest was probably added about 1600 when its use changed to that of an almshouse. It is only 10 feet wide, with massive beams, hence the use of the word 'toy'.

The church of St. Nicholas, begun in the 12th century, has features of almost every century since, including a lectern carved by a local craftsman to celebrate Queen Victoria's Jubilee.

A grisly relic was discovered in the church in 1865, during a major restoration. A human skull was found resting on a roof beam, and it was conjectured that this was of Sir Hector Maclean who fought for the Young Pretender in 1715, and sought sanctuary in the church. Perhaps during the final chase a gun was fired at or in the church, because a bullet hole is said to be still discoverable, although I have been given different locations for it.

December 26th, St. Stephen's Day or Boxing Day, seems to have been a very popular day for cruel hunts or chases in Sussex. Itchingfield was one of the villages which had a squirrel hunt on this particular day of the year. Many people travelled from neighbouring villages to take part in the 'sport' which was known, for some unaccountable reason, as 'skug'. The hunted were brought down from the trees by lead-weighted projectiles.

Keymer ﷼

Older folk call it Kymer, although this pronunciation seems to be giving way to the more obvious one. Lying athwart the border between East and West Sussex, some residents claim to live in one and some in the other. It is a small neat village, with no particular excitements. This is peaceful country and it seems appropriate that the inscription chosen for the memorial to those who fell in the First World War should run:

> 'When peace dawns over the countryside,
> Our thanks shall be to the lads who died.'

A guide published in the early part of this century gives wheat, oats, beans, peas and turnips as the main crops grown in the parish, and it is not surprising that the commercial directory for the same period has a preponderance of gardeners and nurserymen.

But things must have been exciting sometimes. Smugglers operated in this area, as indeed they did in most parts of Sussex, inland as well as the coast. In 1777 the Excise Officer from Horsham, with six dragoons, seized smuggled goods to the value of £5,000 near Keymer. A truly large amount in those days.

Oldlands Post Mill is thought to have been built in the 17th century. It was last worked at the end of the First World War, and in 1927 came into the care of the Sussex Archaeological Society, which raised the money to buy the land on which it stood with the help of a campaign carried out by *The Times* newspaper. The paper described the mill as 'this prominent feature of old England'.

The Keymer Brick and Tile Company was established in 1875 by Samuel Copestake. A local paper commented 'a very large trade appears to have resulted almost instanter'. The hand made tiles and bricks have been used in many well known

114

buildings throughout England, including St. James Church, Piccadilly; and Manchester Central Station.

During the 20th century, production methods have been modernised where possible, although the character of the product is unaltered and the company is still proud of its present-day Keymer Hand Made Clay Tiles. The tiles, although not cheap, have proved to be very popular in modern building, and there is no shortage of satisfied customers. Each year the company holds an open day, and members of the workforce carry out their usual duties voluntarily, watched by inquisitive members of the public. All proceeds of these open days go to a designated charity.

A very interesting sound and slide show has been produced to professional standards, and is popular with the visitors. Included on the recordings are some of the older members of the work-people, who recall with typical Sussex voices, the changes which they have seen at the works through the years.

Kingsfold 🎵

This almost-in-Surrey village was a popular stopping place for charabancs and coaches on summer outings, and evening and mystery tours. Several photographs I have of the Wheatsheaf, from the 1920s, show 'nigger minstrels' entertaining the passengers before they proceeded on their way.

Ralph Vaughan Williams collected a version of the *Horn Fair Song* in this inn on 23rd December 1904. I wonder whether his informant (sometimes given as Ted Gill, and sometimes Teal) was in a seasonal mood. The Kingsfold song is very similar to that sung at Ebernoe fair, but there is an added final verse, making five in all:

> 'There were the finest of horns as ever you did behold,
> There were the finest horns as were gilded with gold;
> And ride, merry, merry, merrily Horn Fair we did go,
> Like jolly, brisk couples, boys, and all in a row.'

115

R.V.W. also collected *The Red Barn* or *The Murder of Maria Martin* at the same time, and used the melody for the hymn *I heard the voice of Jesus say* – calling the tune *Kingsfold*.

Kirdford 🦋

The *Degradation of Drunkenness.*

There is no sin which doth more deface God's image than drunkenness it dispuiseth a person and doth, even, unman him Drunkenness makes him have the throat of a fish the belly of a swine and the head of an ass. Drunkenness is the shame of nature, the extinguisher of reason, the shipwreck of chastity and the murderer of conscience. Drunkenness is hurtful to the body, the cup kills more than the cannon it causes dropsies, catarrhs, apoplexies it fills the eye with fire, and the legs with water and turns the body into an hospital

Stone set in the vicarage wall
Kirdford

This is fruit growing country, and of course the apple trees were wassailed in the days immediately following Christmas. In 1977 The Broadwood Morris men from Horsham revived the old custom, baptising the trees at Redlands Farm with Sussex cider, and tying toast to the branches as a peace offering to the tree spirits. Guns, including an antique from 1830, were fired into the trees, to flush the evil one out, and the men chanted the traditional rhymes encouraging the apples to appear in plenty in

116

due season. One of the moving spirits in the revival of the wassailing custom, was the manager of Kirdford Growers, one of the largest apple suppliers in the country.

George Hugh Kenyon, with four others, formed Kirdford Growers in 1928, as an apple growing co-operative – a very courageous thing to do in view of the economic state of the country at that period. He was also very interested in the glass industry which had strong connections with Kirdford history. In 1967 his book *The Glass Industry of the Weald of Surrey and Sussex* was published, and this has remained the definitive book on the subject. His keen interest in local affairs and the traditional glass makers came together when he provided a lancet window for Kirdford and Wisborough Green churches, each glazed with local glass.

Local glass also features in the lovely village sign, which was erected to commemorate the coronation of King George VI and Queen Elizabeth. It is mounted on a stone plinth, with the name Kirdford worked in open ironwork. Above the name is a diamond of local glass; something which is probably unique in village signs.

There is so much to write about concerning Kirdford, that it is more a question of what must be left out. One thing which must be mentioned is the marvellous plaque on a wall in the centre of the village. This is the message inscribed upon it:

> 'Degradation of Drunkenness. There is no sin which doth more deface God's image than drunkenness. It disguiseth a person and doth even unman him. Drunkenness makes him have the throat of a fish, the belly of a swine and the head of an ass. Drunkenness is the shame of nature, the extinguisher of reason, the shipwreck of chastity and the murderer of conscience. Drunkenness is hurtful to the body, the cup kills more than the cannon. It causes dropsies, catarrhs, apoplexies. It fills the eye with fire, and the legs with water and turns the body into an hospital.'

As may be expected there are several stories connected with the plaque. One is that an unknown villager pushed the text under the vicarage door in the middle of the 19th century. The vicar thought it appropriate as a warning to the drinkers in the Black Bear, and had it inscribed in stone and set up for all to see. Another reason for its existence is said to be that it was one of several such temperance plaques produced in the mid-1800s. It was meant, not so much as warning to the drinkers in the pubs, but as a complaint against the brewers of home-made beer, which was often much stronger than that sold in the pubs. Another story is that far from being erected by the vicar, it was the villagers who had it put up as an admonition to the cleric, who they thought was too much addicted to the temptations of the devil drink. The original stone was damaged in several places, and the one we see today is a facsimile, but at least a unique village curiosity has been preserved.

Kirdford has its share of ghosts and witches. There is a legend about a piece of ground where no grass will grow – because it is said, the blood of a poacher was spilt there. Margaret Cooper lived in the village in the 16th century, and was indicted for murder by witchcraft. She was accused of bewitching three people, all of whom subsequently died. She was found guilty and sentenced to death by hanging.

While in a sombre mood, here is the wording on a Kirdford tombstone, from the grave of five young lads who died in 1838.

> 'To the memory of George Newman, aged 17,
> Charles Newman, aged 13, Thomas Rapley, aged
> 14, George Puttick, aged 13 and William Boxall,
> aged 19 years who died at Sladeland on the 21st of
> January, 1838, from having placed green wood
> ashes in their bedroom. In the midst of life we are
> in death.'

The tragic story behind the inscription tells that the five lads were employed at Sladelands, as houseboys. They slept in a bedroom without a chimney, but often took a bucket of hot ashes from beneath the brick oven where the bread had been baked, up to their room for warmth. A broken window , which had acted as ventilation, had been repaired one day without their knowledge, and so the fumes suffocated them during the night. The story was often told locally, followed by the moral

'Mind you never light a fire in a bucket or you may wake up dead.'

At the funeral of the five unfortunate boys, the bearers most probably wore white smocks. This was the normal custom at Sussex country funerals up until the early years of this century. It is recorded that the six bearers at a funeral at Kirdford as late as 1928 were all dressed in this fashion, possibly the last time this mode of dress was used in this area.

About 1912 the then vicar of Kirdford, Rev. Birrell, was delighted when the local blacksmiths 'fired the anvil' to celebrate his daughter's marriage. (This meant putting gunpowder in holes underneath the anvil, and lighting a trail of powder with a heated rod, to produce a very satisfactory explosion.) George Carley who was present, recalled how the bang shook the forge and covered him with soot, but the vicar had sent down some beer, which soon helped to clear the blacksmiths' throats.

Another old Kirdford custom was revived in 1983, when the Harvest Supper was held in the Parish Hall, and thoroughly enjoyed by many villagers present.

Lindfield ﾞ

Mus' Penfold's ABC of Lindfield

A be the ancient church of the people.
B be the bells that rings in the steeple.
C be the Common where cricketers play.
D be the ducks in the pond on the way.
E be the eggs in the nestes we spies.
F be the Fair and the coconut shies.
G be the grass plots tidy and neat.
H be the high trees that shadders the street.
I be the ins and the outs of the places.
J be the jokes and the jobs that we faces.
K be King Edward's Memory Hall.
L be the lectures, an' concerts, an' ball.
M be the mill and the miller a -grindin'.
N be the neighbours and gossip a-findin'.

O be Ol Place and the ol'-fashion houses.
P be Pax Hill an' pastures where cows is.
Q be the quires that sings in the churches.
R be the river with trouts an' the perches.
S be the signboards that swing in the wind.
T be Town Hill where the houses begin.
U be the uplands for ketching the breeze.
V be the views of the hollers an' trees.
W for waits that shivers and sings.
X be the Xmas tidin's they bring.
Y be the yield of the crops in the season.
Z to be sure there be nothin' in reason.

A dialect poem by an unknown 19th century rhymester, neatly summing up many of the attractions of this beautiful village.

Lindfield has a very long, but pleasing main street, with the (mainly) 13th century church of St. John the Baptist at one end, and the village pond and common at the other. This is truly the archetypal Sussex village, deserving of the many compliments it has received through the years, for its simple but dignified character.

The pond is quite large, four-fifths of an acre, and highly decorative, with the surroundings nicely kept and the water fowl adding colour and movement. Believe it or not, the welfare of the pond is traditionally watched over by a 'Harbour Master' – surely the only gentleman with such a title in any inland village in the county.

Fairs have always been held on the Common, and the August Sheep Fair was one of the largest in the area. The sheep were driven in from all around, and a Sussex newspaper of 1858 spoke of 7,000 sheep and lambs being penned, plus two to three hundred head of other stock. One lady told me of her memories of Lindfield Fair, when she said it always rained. 'You could bank of having to wear wellingtons and having to plod through mud and layers of straw'. Her mother remembered when large flocks of sheep passed through Chailey on the way to Lindfield Fair in the 1880s, raising clouds of dust as they trotted by the Kings Head.

The Village Benefit Friendly Society, founded in 1757, had

two feasts a year, members paying sixpence each for drinks and the same for the meal. For preaching a sermon at the feast, the clergyman received half-a-guinea, and members paid one penny if they interrupted another during the proceedings. There were also other forfeits imposed on members at other times – one shilling if they failed to attend the funeral of a fellow-member, or two shillings and sixpence if they attended the funeral 'in liquor'.

There is an intriguing inscription on a tombstone in the churchyard. The grave is that of Richard Turner who died in 1768, age 21:

> 'Long was my pain, great was my grief
> Surgeons I'd many, but no relief,
> I trust through Christ to rise with the just,
> My leg and thigh was buried fust'.

The Lindfield local historian, Helena Hall, was so pleased to see the use of a dialect word in the epitaph, that she had the inscription re-cut in order to preserve the wording.

We also owe Helena Hall a great debt for expanding and illustrating *A Dictionary of Sussex Dialect,* originally compiled by the Rev. W.D. Parish of Selmeston in 1875. She also wrote a book about William Allen, the Quaker (*William Allen 1770-1843.* 1954). Allen had been associated with Wilberforce in the movement to abolish slavery, and with Elizabeth Fry in the reform of the prison system. He followed these activities with an even more daunting task; that of improving the lot of the English agricultural worker. As a pilot scheme, two farms were procured at Lindfield, and three sets of cottages (six in each set) were built to rent at three shillings, two shillings and sixpence and two shillings respectively a week. Each cottage had a piece of land of one or two acres attached to it. This collection of model cottages soon became known as 'The Colony', and so a unique social experiment came to Lindfield. The story as told in Miss Hall's book is a brave one, and although William Allen was not originally a Sussex man, he spent the latter part of his life in Lindfield and earned a great reputation for sincerity and honesty. His name continued to live on in the well known firm of chemists, Allen and Hanbury, of which he was the main partner.

Littlehaven 🌿

Really just a part of Roffey, Littlehaven has a small railway station (or halt as it used to be called) on the main Victoria – Horsham line, much used by commuters who live in the many neat new houses which now occupy the space of the green fields of my youth. As a schoolboy I played in the fascinating yards of a nearby farm, ate the strawberries in season, or when it rained sat in one of the barns listening to the grandfather telling stories or singing his one song. In those days the halt seemed little used, except on the rare occasions when a party of hikers descended upon it.

Down the road was the school I attended, once a private house and now once again filling that role. The schoolmaster was part local celebrity, part local eccentric. When he was not catching the ends of his dusty black gown in the fire, or fueding with the Catholic priest, he would be riding his big upright cycle around the country lanes hoping (or so it seemed) to catch us boys up to some mischief – which was probably not difficult. As the school grew less prosperous, so the furniture gradually disappeared. Returning after each holiday we would conjecture on the state of the classrooms. Eventually only the teacher's own living room was furnished and heated, and so all the lessons took place there. The pupils sat on the arm chairs and a settee, if they were lucky, or on the floor, if not. For his mid-day meal he partook of an old Sussex dish known as Kettle Broth. This is crumbled bread, with pepper and salt, in a basin of hot water. This the teacher ate standing up, usually holding forth on some topic to me, as I consumed my packed lunch at a bare table (I was the only child who stayed at school during the lunch time). I appreciated the pearls of wisdom floating down on me, but not the drops of water and stray bread that tended to accompany them from time to time.

Lower Beeding 🌿

A village on the edge of St. Leonards Forest, 4½ miles south east of Horsham. Not to be confused with Upper Beeding, which is about ten miles away towards the coast. This area is full of folklore connected with the forest, its iron-smelting history and the hammer ponds.

Holy Trinity church was built as recently as 1840, a copy of Littlemore near Oxford, and therefore very un-Sussex-like in appearance.

Nearby are the 80 acre gardens of Leonardslee, which are open to the public at certain times during the Spring and Autumn. The gardens are nationally famous for their rhododendrons and azaleas, and once had the doubtful added attraction of a number of the small kangaroo like wallabies, in an enclosed portion of the grounds.

The garden was begun in 1889 by Sir Edmund Loder, although some of the conifers date from about 1830. It was entirely Sir Edmund's own work, and no professional designer had a hand in it. The hammer ponds provide a series of small lakes, which add greatly to the incredible views from the terrace of the house.

In a far corner of the garden is a memorial stone made out of an old Sussex millstone and local ripple sandstone. It was erected in memory of Sir Edmund Loder, as it was here he frequently sat when planning his garden.

Lowfield Heath 🦜

Lowfield Heath on the Sussex-Surrey border is a ghost village. Now almost the only building of any size is the church of St. Michael, which still remains rather incongruously. All the rest, the old cottages, the school, the village hall, the blacksmith's, the White Lion, all have gone to be replaced by the noise of the jets from nearby Gatwick Airport.

As a boy I remember cycling over from Horsham to the old Gatwick flying club, with its little bee-hive control building (which still remains) hoping to see a plane actually taking off or landing. There also the racecourse, with a pretty bandstand, which has now found a permanent home in Crawley's Queen's Square.

The old village had plenty of history. A quoits match was played outside the White Lion each Good Friday, and later this became a popular stopping place for motor coaches, with as many as forty or fifty there at one time. A windmill ground grain for the village, and the children went to a little school, where the teacher was pushed each day in a bath chair because of bad health.

Now all this is no more, and all that remains of the old village is in the memories of the older folk who moved away.

Loxwood 🦋

In 1820 John Sirgood was born at Avening in Gloucestershire. As a young man he joined The Plumstead Peculiers, a tiny religious sect preaching faith healing, founded by James Bridges in 1836.

Sirgood became a preacher in London, and one night around 1850 he was told in a dream of certain villages in Sussex where his message was needed. The following day he closed up his shoemaking shop, and with his wife in a wheelbarrow, set out on the forty-odd mile trek from London to Loxwood.

A group of about five people formed around him, and although there were plenty who jeered, in about ten years he had won about half the population of the village over to this teachings. This soon led to violent opposition from local landowners and clergy, and Cokelers – as members of his sect were known – were evicted from tied cottages and denied employment. The real name of the group was The Christian Dependents – the nickname Cokelers was coined because, it was said, of the cocoa which the members consumed at their meetings.

It was not an easy life, but Sirgood's followers believed that they were favoured people, having chosen Christ instead of the pleasures of the world. A verse from a hymn in the Cokelers' hymn book, makes this point clearly:

> 'Though in this world we take our place,
> As other mortals do,
> We're all imbued by him with grace,
> And he will see us through.'

The men and women who embraced these teachings gave up

many things: secular music and books, games, tobacco and alcohol. Marriage although not forbidden, was not part of the Dependent's doctrine. Sirgood owed some of his success to his reputation in Sussex as a healer, although he refused to make this an integral part of his creed.

By 1870 the sect built a chapel at Loxwood, holding three services there each Sunday, and two during the week. At the same time a cemetery was established, and a shop opened. The shop and others which followed in neighbouring villages, was a very important part of the Cokelers' activities. Many of the young women in the sect, who in normal 'service' would have been unable to take part in the religious life, worked instead in the shops, and those with savings invested them in the business. The Cokelers are hard working, thrifty and extremely honest, and for many years the group flourished, and chapels and stores were opened in several other Sussex villages, including Northchapel, Kirdford and Warnham.

But eventually the relatively small sect shrank, and the chapels became used by very small numbers and the shops were closed. Having met some of them, I can say that they are delightfully sincere and unassuming people, and I am sorry that soon the Cokelers will be part of history in West Sussex.

Lurgashall 🦜

Lurgashall, pronounced Lurgasale, is a pleasant unassuming village with a triangular green and the simple but attractive church of St. Laurence. An unusual feature of the latter is the 16th century timber gallery built onto the south wall of the nave. It is said that this was originally a shelter for parishioners coming from a distance, so that they could stay and eat their Sunday dinner in the dry and warmth. Later the gallery became the village school, and still later the vestry.

There was once a church band led by George Sadler, who was such a mainstay that after his death in 1838, the band soon faded away. K.H. McDermott in his *Sussex Church Music in the Past* (1922) quotes the local comment that the band was 'never no sense afterwards'. The singing continued without musical accompaniment; 'someone used to start a tune and the rest on us came in'.

One of the rectors was James Bramston, author of *The Art of Politics*. His excellent advice to public speakers was –

'Those who would captivate the well-bred throng,
Should not too often speak, nor speak too long'.

I wonder if he followed his own adage when in the church pulpit.

Lurgashall lies at the foot of Blackdown, and here died an even more famous literary figure, Lord Tennyson.

Lyminster

The little village of Lyminster near Arundel, is a great place for legends. It has a ghost, a secret tunnel and perhaps best of all, a dragon.

The ghost story concerns a nun who was said to haunt the ancient church. A Saxon Nunnery once stood where there is now a farm. The Nunnery was refounded after the Conquest but was finally suppressed by Henry VIII.

The tunnel also had connections with the nuns; it was supposed to run between Calcete Priory and Lyminster Nunnery, a distance of 1½ miles – a relatively short tunnel compared to many others in Sussex legend.

Not far from the church of St. Mary Magdalene is the mysterious Nucker or Knucker Hole. The traditionally held belief is that this and other similar ponds are bottomless. Many years ago the six bell ropes of the church were knotted together, and dropped down into the hole, but did not reach the bottom. At least that is the story, although a more modern and less romantic version has it that the pond is in fact about 30 feet deep. The water is always cool in summer, but never freezes in the winter. In the *Sussex Dialect Dictionary*, Nucker Holes are described as 'springs which rise in the flat lands of the South Downs.....are found at Lyminster, Lancing, Shoreham, Worthing.....' so in this respect Lyminster is not unique.

However, the Lyminster Nucker Hole has attached to it a particularly persistent legend of a fierce and frightening

126

dragon. The Anglo-Saxon word Nicon meant sea-monster, so it seems reasonable to assume that the dragon story goes back to Anglo-Saxon times.

As is usual in these legends, the culmination is the slaying of the dragon, in this case existing as a separate story in several different versions. Some say that it was the King of Sussex who offered his lovely daughter's hand in marriage to anyone who could destroy the Nucker. A wandering knight engaged the reptile in combat, and vanquished it. He married the princess and they lived happily in Lyminster for the rest of their lives.

Another more interesting version tells of a local lad, Jim Puttock, who prepared a huge pudding, which he offered to the dragon. The greedy monster gobbled it all up much too quickly, and was overcome by indigestion, whereupon Jim cut off its head with his axe. This story was printed in Sussex dialect in the *Sussex County Magazine* in 1929.

Other similar variants speak of the people of Lyminster preparing the pudding and offering it to the creature, which was 'green, greasy and scaly', on a long skewer-like pole. It stuck in the dragon's throat and the villagers were able to pull the monster out, and chop him up. A correspondent in a Sussex newspaper in 1965 suggested that this tale bore similarities to the method once used in East Africa to kill crocodiles.

Then there are those who believe that the dragon-slayer was not Jim Puttock but Jim Pulk, who baked a huge pie with poison in it, and carried it on a Sussex cart close to the Nucker Hole. The dragon smelt it, came out and devoured pie, cart, horse and all, subsequently dying of the poison. Jim Pulk cut off its head with his scythe, going to the Six Bells for a celebratory drink. Sadly he later fell down dead, having somehow got some of the poison on his hand, which he drew across his mouth at the end of his drink.

Another more matter-of-fact explanation was offered some years ago, to the effect that the Nucker was a huge eagle. One version of the more traditional story (printed in the *Sussex Archaeological Collections* of 1866) does speak of the dragon 'flying with inconceivable rapidity through the air'.

But surely no-one can doubt the story of the dragon-slayer when his tombstone can still be seen in the church. It is a medieval stone slab, without inscription but with a worn design of a cross superimposed on a herring-bone pattern. The stone once lay outside the church, but has been moved into the church to preserve it.

Madehurst

E.V. Lucas called it 'one of the most remote of Sussex villages'. That was in 1904, and even today the local Women's Institute admits, albeit with a certain pride, 'We are just a simple country hamlet set in beautiful countryside, heavily wooded. Peace and quiet and walks are all we offer'. Nairn and Pevsner in *The Buildings of England-Sussex* (1965) embellish this description slightly by describing Madehurst as 'not a village, just a scattered handful of 19th century estate cottages, two of them flanking the church formally', and they also comment on the magnificent setting and the remoteness. Not surprisingly a part of the parish bears the name 'No Man's Land'.

Madehurst is rather special to me, as it was here, when visiting Madehurst Lodge that I met George Belton. George helped to manage the small farm, and had all the attributes of the finest type of countryman. He was completely natural and unselfconscious with a kindly sense of humour and vast store of songs and stories, particularly the former. He had worked with horses most of his life on different farms in Sussex and Surrey. Born in 1898, the youngest of a family of five, he was always of small stature and was often teased about his lack of inches. This was particularly so on the day when he took a pair of horses from a farm at the bottom of Clayton Hill, up to a field close to the Jack and Jill windmills. The wind was blowing, and because of his smallness George found he just hadn't the strength to shut the gate leading into the field. So he took the trace horse and hooked him on to the end of the gate, so that the horse pulled it shut.

He was a champion ploughman and won over eighty prizes in ploughing matches, so his lack of height was no drawback where work on the farm was concerned.

I remember the January day in 1967, when with a colleague I set up recording gear in the dining room of Madehurst Lodge, in order to record some of George's songs for an L.P. This was obviously a unique experience for him, but he was completely placid about the whole thing, and sailed through every song without a hitch. Many times I had helped in recording professional and experienced performers, but never had a recording session gone so easily and smoothly.

He was always remembering songs that he had learnt in his youth, during the years I knew him. One day he heard another singer perform a very ancient song *The Bold Fisherman* and he remarked to me 'I used to know that song years ago'. The next time we met he had remembered the complete song, and was able to sing it to me with ease.

As well as the traditional songs which he had learnt over the years from family and friends, he was always willing to learn something new if it took his fancy. Sydney Carter, composer of *Lord of the Dance* was delighted when he heard George sing his *Mixed Up Old Man*. I shall never forget hearing George's honest country tones merging with the more polished voices of the daughters of the family for whom he worked – more as a friend than an employee – in a version of the carol *Masters in this Hall* which they had taught him.

Mannings Heath

Whenever I talk to people about the past in Mannings Heath, they invariably comment on how much walking was done. One lady said 'Everyone walked everywhere at that time'. Another commented 'How the folk walked in those days'.

One informant's grandfather was the superintendent of the Sunday School, walking from Nuthurst where he lived to Mannings Heath every Sunday morning, with his two young children. They took their dinner with them and stayed to afternoon Sunday school and service, before walking back to Nuthurst for tea. After tea he walked to Horsham for the evening service.

Another man rose each morning at 4.30 in order to walk from Mannings Heath to Cowfold, three miles away, for his work. All the children walked to school of course, and even fetching the water could involve walking. One well served a line of cottages, and the cottagers at the far end of the line had quite a long way to walk to reach the well – although one lady considered it a treat to be allowed to accompany her grandfather when he went to fetch the water.

A Methodist church was started in the village in the mid-19th century, built on land bought for five pounds. One lady accompanied her aunt when she cleaned the church, helping her to fill little oil lamps on the walls. The seats faced towards a big oil-fashioned stove in the centre of the chapel.

There is a popular inn in the village, the Dun Horse, replacing an earlier one of the same name which was demolished in the 1920s. One man told me how he had been brought up there, and how all the drink was kept in the cellars which were under water each winter. The pub had a little shop at one end, and his mother looked after this. It was hard work, open early and late, and until 11.00 pm on Saturday. No one was paid until 5.00 or 6.00 pm on Saturdays, so most of the weekly shopping had to be done on Saturday nights when folk had some money.

Another memory was of a spring of clear water, perfect for quenching one's thirst. Then there was 'Idle Corner', where the young folk used to idle their evenings away. The younger children looked forward eagerly to the annual visit of the toy seller, who brought a truck containing all kinds of penny items – sweets, toffee apples, kites and many more.

Back in the 18th-century, John Fuller, a successful smuggler lived at Mannings Heath. His obvious business was broom-dashing and charcoal burning, but he also received large quantities of contraband spirits from the coast, which he sold concealed in bundles of brooms and broom sticks – which were really just the ends, with the middle hollowed out. The old man travelled the country around in his horse and cart, selling brooms and charcoal to his innocent customers, and brandy and other spirits to those in the know. He is supposed to have died owning a large amount of property, having amassed a small fortune by his secondary occupation.

The Mardens ✒

Four villages that go North, East, West and Up. The first two and the last have churches, although West Marden without a church is actually the biggest village. Tradition has it that it was here that St. Richard of Sussex worked a minor miracle and provided the villagers with a spring of clear water, in answer to their prayers. Now even their church has disappeared.

All three churches are worth visiting, but St. Mary's at North Marden is of particular interest in being one of the smallest in Sussex. Portsmouth is only fifteen miles away, but the villages seem as quiet and remote as any in Sussex; although perhaps not as quiet as in 1861 when the population of North Marden was but 28.

Middleton ﹩

One of several coastal villages, to the east of Bognor Regis. It has suffered greatly from inroads of the sea, in fact the present small church of St. Nicholas was built in 1849, to replace the older one which was being destroyed by the waves. An account of the original church as it looked in 1835, gives some idea of how the process of erosion took place:

> 'The South aisle, tower and half the chancel with
> the whole South side of the churchyard, have been
> absorbed and are now covered with shingle. The
> latter is entirely desolate, not having retained a
> single memorial of the dead'.

It has been stated that medical students around this time found the devastated churchyard a useful source of supply for human bones.

By 1883 a further eye-witness description of the same, spoke of 'a mass of debris – a mixture of earth and shingle, with bricks, chalk and black logs of wood, the remains of shattered groynes'.

One would expect such a place to provide many stories of ghosts and spectres, and I found this one in *Glimpses of our Sussex Ancestors. Volume 11* (1883). It concerns a friend of the writer who was returning from a shooting expedition late one moonlight night. When he reached the ruins of Middleton church he was startled to see an object in front of the church wall, in the shape of a human form with threatening out-

131

stretched arms. He raised his gun and shouted 'Speak or I'll fire'. He was just about to give the 'ghost' a charge of No.1 duck-shot, when a voice from a neighbouring groyne asked him what he was doing, and implored him not to 'pepper my great coat'. The owner of the voice was a coastguardsman, who had hung his wet coat to dry on the old church wall.

Middleton's best known real ghost story is about a Headless Horseman, a smuggler, who is supposed to haunt Ashmere Lane. Gerard Young, who wrote about Flansham and the surrounding countryside in the 1940s, gave more details in *The Cottage in the Fields* (1945). On one occasion one man saw the ghostly rider on the side of the road. He described the horse as real, but the rider as a spectre. The man flung two pint bottles of beer at the apparition, which it was felt proved that there must have been something there! When this story was recounted in The Fox at Felpham, someone looked up casually and said 'Yes, he's still around. Been seen about six weeks ago'.

Headless Horsemen must be some of the most common ghosts in Sussex, and the replacement of horses by mechanical means of transport does not seem to have banished them. Another well-known type of story, usually associated with witches, is echoed in a further Middleton tale. Four men with a two-horse wagon were journeying from Middleton to Slindon to fetch wood. They were not far out of the village, when the two horses suddenly stopped dead, shivering and with the sweat running down their bodies. The mens swore, whipped them, and did everything they could think of to make them move, but all to no avail. Suddenly there was the sound as of a heavy chain being dragged across the road, and the horses immediately recovered their composure and pulled the wagon over the haunted spot.

Yet another local ghost story tells of 'The Grey Lady', who is supposed to haunt Ancton Manor.

Monks Gate 🦊

Most books on Sussex overlook Monks Gate, although the village's name was permanently commemorated by Ralph Vaughan Williams in *The English Hymnal* which he edited in

1906.

Monks Gate was the name he attached to the tune of the folk song *Our Captain calls all hands* or *Fountains flowing* which he collected from Mrs. Harriet Verrall of that place in 1904.

> 'Our Captain calls all hands to sail tomorrow,
> Leaving my dear to mourn in grief and sorrow,
> 'Dry up those briny tears, and leave off weeping,
> So happy may we live at our next meeting.'

The song tells of a young man who is about to sail away, presumably to war, despite the entreaties of his sweetheart. After arrangement by Ralph Vaughan Williams the tune of this traditional song was fitted to words by John Bunyan, and became well known as *The Pilgrim's Hymn.*

> 'He who would valiant be 'gainst all disaster,
> Let him in constancy follow the Master,
> There's no discouragement, shall make him once relent,
> His first avowed intent, to be a pilgrim'.

Mr. & Mrs. Verrall, Peter and Harriet, lived in Nuthurst Road, Monks Gate, later moving to North Street in Horsham, and then to Stanley Street, Horsham. Mrs. Verrall seemed to possess the largest store of songs, although her husband was also a singer, and they often sang to each other for their own pleasure in the evenings.

As well as the wonderful tune used by Vaughan Williams for *The Pilgrim's Hymn,* Mrs. Verrall also gave the composer the even better known *Sussex Carol;* also in 1904.

> 'On Christmas night all Christians sing,
> To hear the news the angels bring,
> On Christmas night all Christians sing,
> To hear the news the angels bring,
> News of great joy, news of great mirth,
> News of our merciful King's birth.'

In 1905 Mrs. Verrall submitted this carol to a competition

sponsored by the Sussex newspaper *The West Sussex Gazette.* She won first prize, not for *The Sussex Carol* but for her versions of two fine traditional songs *Covent Garden* and *Salisbury Plain,* both of which she had already sung to Ralph Vaughan Williams in the previous year. The adjudicator of the competition was Miss Lucy Broadwood of Rusper, secretary of the Folk Song Society at that time.

The Verralls are buried in an unmarked grave in Hills Cemetery, Horsham, Harriet having died in 1918 at about 63 and Peter a few years later. Although they ended their lives in Horsham, they will be remembered as the singers from Monks Gate, mainly due to Vaughan Williams' habit of naming hymn tunes after the villages where he collected them.

Northchapel ෨෧

So named, we are told, because the chuch was once a chapelry, north of Petworth. Until very recently, it was spelled as two separate words, North and Chapel.

The roads in this area were once infamous, and several stories exist of famous personages taking many hours travelling the last few miles through Northchapel on their way to Petworth. Later the roads were made up with local ironstone, and a brick built toll house was provided at Northchapel. Included in the usual list of tolls for pedestrians, horse drawn vehicles, horses, cattle, sheep and so on was a penny charge for any truck, barrow, or other carriage drawn by a dog. The toll house ceased to function in 1871, when most of the road tolls were abolished.

Apart from passing traffic, this is now a quiet, peaceful part of Sussex, and it is difficult to believe that it was once in the centre of the thriving glass and iron industries. In the 19th century a charcoal manufactory was established close to the village, with a daily consumption of fifteen hundredweight of wood. Northchapel poultry keepers were famous for their fowls, and of course for many centuries the area has been known as apple growing country.

Although Sussex is no longer normally regarded as a cider-producing county, some of the best cider obtainable was once produced in this neighbourhood – not to be sold, but almost all

Goffs Farm, Northchapel

of it consumed at home. Hardiman Scott in his *Secret Sussex* (1949) wrote of a renowned cider maker, Jim Bicknell, a besom broom maker, who lived about a mile west of Northchapel.

Most cider makers are credited with adding a little something to their brew, and I am sure the Northchapel cider men were no exception. A popular country joke is to accuse a cider maker of adding a dead rat along with the apples. This I am sure was just a bit of rustic fun, but I am not so certain about other things, such as a bit of raw meat.

Northchapel and cricket are connected due to the Sussex cricketer, Noah Mann, who was born here in 1756. He was the landlord of the Half Moon Inn, riding the twenty miles to Hambledon to practise with that famous club, once a week. He was an all round sportsman, and one of his feats was to pick up handkerchiefs from the ground when riding his horse at full speed. With permission, he named his son, Horace, after the cricketing baronet Sir Horace Mann. He died at the age of 33, after falling into his own pub fire, when asleep following a tiring day's shooting. He is buried in the churchyard.

In more modern times, the village had another celebrity as a resident, the First World War artist, Bruce Bairnsfather, creator of that wonderful character Old Bill.

Some of the old cures noted from the past were almost worse than the complaints they were supposed to treat. One of the nastiest was recorded at Northchapel by Charlotte Latham in her *Some West Sussex Superstitions lingering in 1868.* A sufferer with weak eyes was recommended to wear a live toad around his neck until dead (the toad – not the patient). He followed the advice, and remarked that he felt a lot better in consequence (the patient – not the toad).

North Stoke ✤

In the spring of 1834, workmen deepening a sewer ditch on a farm in the parish of North Stoke discovered, about six feet down, an ancient boat formed from a hollowed-out tree trunk; rather like an Indian canoe.

It measured 34 feet 6 inches in length, and 4 feet 6 inches wide at the centre. The depth was 2 feet 6 inches in the centre. There were three compartments, serving as seats and to strengthen the craft. No one has dared to date it, but one writer described it as 'older than history.'

Nuthurst ✤

Although but four miles from busy Horsham, little Nuthurst is still very much a country village. There is the much restored church of St. Andrew; one of the few which once used a drum as an accompaniment to its choir. There are also a number of fine old buildings, including the 16th century Black Horse inn, with an adjoining terrace of cottages.

A pamphlet written by H.P. Clark early in the 19th century, gives a glimpse of harvest customs in Nuthurst during the years 1812-1813. The farmer was called 'Maister' and his wife 'Dame'. When the last load of corn was ready, the bells were put on the horses, and when the last sheaf was pitched, the health of the farmer and his wife was drunk by all the workers, which included additional help from the village. The harvest supper, generally on the same night, consisted of old English food, followed by ale and tobacco. The first toast was always to 'The Maister – the founder of the feast'. The toasts were mainly in song, and the second one was to the 'Dame'.

'Now we've drunk our Maister's health,
We will drink our Dame's.
We'll drink and be merry, boys,
In drinking the same:
For him we've drunk one glass,
For her we'll drink two,
We'll drink and be merry, boys,
Before we all go'.

Next came the forfeit game of 'Turning the Bowl'. Each member of the company in turn drank from a horn cup held in a bowl, while the rest sang. The empty cup was then thrown in the air, and the bowl turned over, before catching the cup. (In some places a hat was used instead of a bowl). Failure to complete the sequence, meant a second attempt as a forfeit. Toasts to the farming boys, the woodcutters, the carters, and other trades meant that there was no excuse for leaving glasses empty. The farming boy's toast was as follows:

'The flail that we do handle,
So lustily we will swing,
And at the harvest supper,
So merrily will sing,
Success unto the farming boys,
Or else you are to blame,
I wish them health and happiness,
Till harvest comes again'.

Queen Elizabeth II's Silver Jubilee was marked in Nuthurst by the publication of a ninety-six page book *Nuthurst 1977*. Although something of the past appears in the book, it is mainly a picture of the village as it existed in 1977 – there is even an account of a daily commuter's journey to London. What a boon it will be to historians of the future.

Oving 🪾

Oving is a very healthy place, at least it was in 1835 when the parish had five inhabitants aged between 80 and 90 and one between 90 and 100, all we are assured in perfect health. Not so noteworthy today, but unusual for the early 19th century.

It lies in the flat land, on one side of Tangmere airfield. The church of St. Andrew would, apart from its tower, be almost indistinguishable from a medieval tithe barn, according to Nairn and Pevsner. It was once one of the Sussex churches which used a barrel-organ for its musical accompaniment. An enormous gallery was erected in 1787 for the church choir, but was removed at the 'restoration' of the church in 1840. Two fields near the church were known as 'bell rope fields', the rent being used to provide bell ropes for the ringers.

Pagham 🪾

Once known locally as Selsey Haven, Pagham was at one time an important port. In the 14th century huge storms caused great changes, and the harbour virtually ceased to exist. All that is now left of the original port is a small basin known as the Lagoon. At full tide the harbour and adjoining fields are covered by water and constitute a nature reserve, attracting a large variety of birds including even very rare species. For those who wish to know more about the natural history of Pagham Harbour, the Bognor Regis Natural Science Society have published two books, part I dealing with birds and mammals, and part II plants, and animals other than birds and mammals.

There is an interesting ancient church, St. Thomas a Becket, which has a modern rose window commemorating the recovery from illness of the late King George V, who convalesced at a house within the parish of Pagham. Bognor, with its appendix Regis, claims the honours, but perhaps discreetly in view of the reported remarks of the King when asked if he would be revisiting the town after his return to health.

Old guide books mention an unusual phenomenon known as

'The Hushing Well'. This was apparently once a great local attraction; not really a well at all, but probably an underground spring in the gravel bed of the lagoon. The noise of bursting bubbles on the surface of the water has been described as like the simmering of a great cauldron.

Much of old Pagham has disappeared, and a number of bungalows, many based on old railway carriages, mushroomed during the inter-war years. Today modern estates provide more aesthetically satisfying dwellings for a great many new residents.

In recent times a new custom has become an annual event. This is the Pagham Pram Race, with dozens of participants racing over a two mile course. Many are in fancy dress with even more fanciful prams, and of course it's all in the aid of charity.

Partridge Green 🦢

The name derives from John Partridge (or Partrych) who owned the green about 1300, and it has been conjectured that his name meant that he was a hunter of partridges, and that therefore this may have been some kind of game reserve.

One old building which no longer remains was Jolesfield Windmill which was a local landmark for about 170 years. The last miller was George Knight, who used to get up in the night to work the mill when the wind was right. The mill became disused at the beginning of the 20th century, when a steam mill started up in the village. The mill, like many others, had a reputation of being haunted; not surprising in view of the many years of neglect when the only occupants were owls. The mill was dismantled in 1959.

In 1980 I visited Partridge Green to call on Roger Clarke who under the name of 'Against the Grain' made traditional toys and crafts by hand. As a schoolmaster he collected old games and toys and became an enthusiast for handmade articles. Then he decided to start making toys as a full time occupation, and with his wife he produced and marketed such games as Solitaire, Fox and Geese, Nine Mens Morris, Horse Shoe, Tic-Tac-Toe and Put and Take. Then there are the games with foreign origins such as Brother Jonathan – an 18th century game from the U.S.A., Tigers and Oxen from Siam, Mu-Torere – a Maori game and Four Field Kono from Korea.

Patching ✺

Sometimes confused with Patcham, which is in East Sussex; this village is about five miles from Worthing, in a most beautiful setting at the foot of the Downs. The woods are ideal for picnicking and camping, and the view from Patching Hill is considered to be one of the finest in Sussex.

Truffles (*Lycoperdon Tuber*) were once prolific in Patching woods. In the 19th century a noted truffle hunter, William Leach, came from the West Indies and worked his way along the coast from Cornwall to the mouth of the Thames. He took four years searching for the best spot for truffles, and at last settled upon Patching. Here he carried on a thriving business as truffle hunter for the rest of his life. That great period for characters, the 19th century, also provided a church-warden at the ancient church of St. John, who was extremely conscientious. One Sunday a local farmer's family were talking and giggling during the service. Sir John Kirkland, the churchwarden, could stand it no longer and decided to remonstrate with them, but to no avail. After a pause, he again crossed to their box pew, opened the door and stood bowing until they left.

Near the village are a group of neolithic flint mines, where over 100 shafts have been found. Folklore has it that the Patching flint mines are the last home of the fairies in England.

For nearly 300 years the Shelleys were at Michelgrove, a vast estate stretching from Poling to Shoreham and taking in Angmering Park. In 1800 it was sold to a Mr Walker of Liverpool, and during his time the house was modernised. In 1828, being unable to maintain it, the Walkers sold out to the Duke of Norfolk, who it was said pulled the building down, lest it should vie with Arundel Castle in grandeur.

A pigeon house was built on the Michelgrove estate about 1760, consisting of two storeys. After 1800, during the Walker's time, a third storey was added to turn the building into a clock

140

tower. When the tower fell into disuse, a dung-cart race was arranged between several neighbouring parishes to see who should take over the clock. The race was won by a Steyning farmer, and that is why Steyning High Street now has such a splendid clock. In the 1940s the army used the area for manoeuvres and the tower was partly demolished. It stood in ruins until the 1950s and by 1970 had become a mere heap of rubble.

Much Patching local history is stored within the covers of a diary kept by the Tompkins family, who were estate agents at Michelgrove in the 18th and early 19th centuries. The diary mentions such things as children being sent to school at Widow Pages; a bull being fattened for distribution on St. Thomas' Day – when the poor and the old were traditionally helped with gifts of food for Christmas; and even more important events such as the fire at Cowdray House.

Some of the foregoing comes from a very brief history *Patching and its Church,* which is undated and anonymous, but nevertheless extremely valuable.

Pease Pottage 🎔

In spite of its intriguing name, Pease Pottage is missing from most books on Sussex – even *Highways and Byways* by E.V. Lucas, which misses very little. According to tradition prisoners on their way to Horsham gaol were allowed to stop here for a bowl of pottage – a mash of boiled dried peas eaten with a piece of pork. Hence the name. Another story has it that the guards of George IV, preceding him on the way to Brighton, used to stop here for a meal of pease pottage. But this cannot be the origin of the name, as it is recorded as Peaspottage Gate as early as 1724; before George IV was born!

Although I doubt if it was the meal given to the unfortunate prisoners on their way to Horsham gaol, here is a recipe for Pease Pottage from an old book in Horsham Museum library:

'Take a quart of strong broth, the flour of half a pint of pease, and an ox-palate, all boil'd tender,

141

clarified and cut in pieces; season all with a little pepper, mace and salt; when it boils, put in a little spearmint, and sorrel a little chopp'd, four balls of forc'd meat green'd, a little white bread-like dice, toasted on a plate before the fire; then put in four ounces of fresh butter; toss it up'.

One of our Sussex folk singers of more recent times was Jim (nicknamed 'Brick') Harber who came to live at Pease Pottage from Worcestershire when he was six years old. He worked in agricultural jobs most of his life, but latterly with the Electricity Board at Crawley. He sang sitting upright, with eyes closed and had what was described as a 'very edgy voice'. He had a large repertoire of songs, and at one time also played the tin whistle.

Two modern stories concerned with Pease Pottage, both involving the M23 motorway which terminates there.

Because the motorway has no stopping places, some people coming from it into Pease Pottage are badly in need of a suitable place to relieve themselves. The village had a shop, but no public convenience, and the shop owner, naturally enough, grew rather tired of coping with desperate folk who pleaded to use his loo. I am not sure if any solution is in the pipeline even now.

Modern Sussex folklore includes many stories of big cats, or more specifically pumas. In 1975, one was seen at Pease Pottage sitting beside the end of the motorway. Looking for a toilet, perhaps!

Plaistow 🦡

Usually pronounced Plasto, E.V.Lucas said that this village is 'on the road to nowhere, and has not its equal for quietude in England.' Possibly rather less quiet today, but still a very comforting, untroubled place. The origin of the name is said to indicate a spot where people gathered to take part in games, although why they chose somewhere as remote as this is not clear.

Plaistow's unique example of folklore is connected with Nell

Holy Trinity Church, Plaistow

Ball, a name which persists in a modern housing estate. A tree
once stood on a mound, known locally as Nell Ball Tree. Such
an unusual name was sure to attract several stories. One is that
the tree was planted by Nell Gwynn, who is supposed to have
stayed at Plaistow Place. Another legend has it that Ellen Ball
was a local lady who committed suicide on the hill. Earl
Winterton writing in the *West Sussex Gazette* in 1959,
dismissed both stories, saying that the tree was more probably
named after Nell Quinnel, who lived at Quinnel House, in the
18th century. The tree could have been planted during her
lifetime and the knoll on which it stood called 'Nell's Knoll',
which later may have been changed into Nell Ball because of the
circular shape of the hill.

Years ago, simple-minded folk lived cheek-by-jowl with
other local people in our Sussex villages, being treated with
gentleness most of the time, although occasionally the butt of

143

school boys, and providing local humourists with some very good stories. Such a one lived at Plaistow about a century ago. 'Silly Jim' earned a few shillings by chopping wood, and took an interest in current happenings. A correspondent in the *Sussex County Magazine* in 1943 told how on hearing that electricity had come to Godalming (about ten miles away), he decided he would walk there and see for himself. When he returned his report was 'I walked all way Godalming see elastic light, an' when I get there it wan' shinin'. It was daytime, of course.

Plummers Plain 🦚

A quaintly named hamlet within the parish of Lower Beeding, once part of St. Leonards Forest with its memories of iron works and hammer ponds. Hammer Pond Cottages, now make one complete and very attractive building, roofed with Horsham stone slabs.

On December 22nd 1904 Ralph Vaughan Williams collected three songs from Ted Baines, a seventy year old cowkeeper at Plummers Plain. One of the three songs was a rare find; a song not otherwise noted from oral tradition (although a version exists on a rare ballad sheet). The song was *All things are quite silent,* a lovely ballad about the press gang. This dreaded institution often featured in folk songs, sometimes long after it was extinct, although Roy Palmer in *Folk Songs Collected by Ralph Vaughan Williams* (1983) suggests that in this case all evidence points to the song being contemporary with the operations of the gang. The song begins:

'All things are quite silent, each mortal at rest,
When me and my true love got snug in our nest.'

It goes on to tell how the press gang entered saying that 'The King wants sailors', and in spite of the singer's entreaties, refusing to leave without their quarry. The last two verses relate how the husband walked with his wife in the fields whilst the birds sang sweetly, and she then goes on to hope that her sailor may return one day so that they can once more live happily together.

144

together.

Near Plummers Plain is the so called 'Money Mound' in a farm field, which was excavated over a period of several months in 1961 mainly by pupils from a Crawley school. Roman coins, some fragments of pottery and lastly the real reason for the excavation, a burial chamber, were found. The reason for the name was said to be because over the years ancient coins had been turned up by rabbits in the vicinity of the mound. A local rhyme was supposed to say 'When the year is turned upside down, then treasure will be found in Money Mound'. And of course several people were quick to point out that 1961 turned upside down, is still 1961.

Poling 🦢

When Phoebe Somers interviewed an ex Poling resident in 1977, he said with conviction 'Poling was the best place in the world to live.'

The village had several characters who remained there all their lives. One of these was Sid Penn, who was the village wheelwright, carpenter and undertaker. It was said that Sid made his own coffin, and then kept his groceries in it. Another story is that he buried the family treasure in the garden when Poling was bombed during the war. Some of his tools are now in Arundel Museum.

Poling is the setting of one of the most persistent ghost stories in Sussex. In the 12th century the Knights Hospitallers of St. John of Jerusalem founded a commandery there. Some of the building is now incorporated into a house known as Fairplace Farm or St. John's Priory. Legend has it that many of the knights were buried in a vault in the grounds. Several people seem to have heard the same sounds on different occasions – that of Gregorian chant concluding with the Gloria Patri. Some have described it as a procession approaching. Someone even wrote down the music and it was later identified as plainsong for a requiem service. Someone else heard the 79th psalm in latin, part of vespers of the medieval community.

Poynings

The 14th century church of The Holy Trinity nestles closely into the Downs; of which the village is really a part. The latter takes its name from the Poynygges, who were the Lords of the Manor, the present church having been built under the will of Michael de Poynygges who died in 1369. His will stated 'Two hundred marcs (£2400) to build a new church at Poynygges.' His wife's will (she died within a few weeks of her husband) included 'To the new building of the church two hundred marcs; to Thomas my son, a hundred marcs until he be of full age, then to be given to the building of the said church'. Of the incumbents, George Beard was rector for probably the longest period, although he is said to have used but two texts for his sermons during the whole time. The rectors who succeeded him found a very neglected church, and from the early 19th century much restoration work was carried out.

Because of Poynings' downland character, shepherds must always have been important personages in the life of the village. Nelson Coppard was one such; born in Poynings in 1863, his father having also been a shepherd in the same area. He earned two shillings and sixpence a week until he became a fully-fledged shepherd, when his wage became twelve shillings a week, plus one and sixpence for his dog. There is much about Nelson and other shepherds of the same period in Barclay Wills' much sought-after book *Shepherds of Sussex* (c. 1938). A lovely photo of Nelson Coppard, taken by the author, appears as a frontispiece in this book. He told Barclay Wills that his usual dress had been 'good corduroy suits and gaiters, with a hard felt 'bowler' hat,' but his father had worn a smock, 'a blue one, not like the slaty-colour one I got for you, but blue – what you might call a butcher blue.' He once remarked to Mr Wills 'I says what I thinks, an' I talks in front of people as I talks behind their backs! If what you thinks be *right,* then what you says will be *right* too!' Wisdom, indeed.

Smugglers must have been active in the area, just as they were once in most of coastal and downland Sussex. A story from Poynings tells of a number of kegs of brandy which were bobbing about just below the surface of the mill-pond, while the revenue men were searching inside the mill. The miller and his wife kept them occupied, while a message was hastily despatched to the upper mill to release the water, so that it might drown the tell-tale kegs!

Mention Poynings to most Sussex people and they will immediately think of Devil's Dyke, which must surely be one of the best known and well written-about spots in our county. The traditional legend concerning it is so well known that I hestitate to re-tell it yet again, but in case any reader has not previously come across our best known folk story, let me say briefly that the account in many slightly differing versions involves the Devil being outwitted in his attempt to drown the churches in the weald, by digging a trench or 'Dyke' to allow the sea to sweep in. His digging provided great lumps of earth and stone which he threw in all directions, thus providing us with Chanctonbury and Cissbury Rings, Rackham Hill, Mount Caburn, the Goldstone at Hove, and even the Isle of Wight!

His attempts were thwarted by either an old woman with a candle, St. Cuthman, St. Dunstan, or some unknown Sussex Saint. Nearby are two mounds known as the Devil's Grave and the Devil's wife's Grave, and it is supposed to be unlucky to walk on them.

There are many Devil stories in Sussex folklore, but none seem to have caught the popular imagination in quite the same way as the accounts of his attempt to flood the weald.

The Dyke is a curved valley some three quarters of a mile in length, which does indeed look like an artificial excavation. The Dyke Hill is about 700 feet in height, and on a fine day provides a splendid view into Sussex, Hampshire, Surrey and Kent. Today cars, coaches and buses take visitors up to the Dyke, but in the early part of the 20th century a railway line from Brighton and Hove ended at the Dyke station. When the railway was being built, a skeleton of a woman was discovered by the navvies, and popular imagination immediately linked this with the woman who thwarted the Devil in his attempts to flood the weald. This was the period of what a book published at the time called *Many Modern Attractions.* There was a mountain railway to ascend or descend the slope of the punch bowl, an aerial railway to travel across it, and a thriving hotel run by Mr James Hubbard – who also organised fairs, bands, gypsy fortune tellers, and even a newspaper *The Devil's Dyke Times.*

147

This cost one penny, had sixteen pages and astonishingly was said to have a circulation of one million. On Whit-Monday 1893 there were no less than 30,000 visitors to the Dyke attractions. One unusual feature, often seen on picture postcards c. 1900, was a huge wooden cannon, apparently with no obvious purpose. *The Devil's Dyke Times* described it all in most glowing terms:

> 'What a delightful spot to spend a happy day!
> What pleasant memories one has of a 'day at the
> Dyke!' .... It is quite safe to say that no pleasure
> resort is patronised by the residents so extensively
> as the Dyke.'

Mr Hubbard had, I suppose, every reason to be satisfied with his efforts, but most visitors today will be more than happy to find Poynings and the Dyke almost as quiet and peaceful as they were in the mid-19th century, before Mr Hubbard provided additional 'attractions'.

The little railway which ran from Brighton to the Dyke on a single track, as well as what a contemporary poster called 'the great cable railway' and 'the steep grade railway', are all well chronicled in the book by Paul Clark *The Railways of Devil's Dyke* (1976).

As I write, sheep are once again back on the Downs near Poynings. The sheep have returned to the Devil's Dyke area as part of a West Sussex County Council project aimed at restoring the downland country to its former condition before the decline of sheep farming.

Pulborough

> 'From Pulboro' to Storrington, and many a league
> around,
> Cuckoo-birds were calling, calling, calling all the
> way,
> Ringing out their shout of love from every hurst
> and thorpe,
> Cuckoo-birds were calling in the may'.

Assuredly cuckoos still call in Pulborough, just as they did when Arthur Bell wrote his poem *From Pulboro' to Storrington,* although much else from the past has faded into oblivion.

Old inhabitants used to talk of the treasure buried under the Mount; and a clergyman often seen digging there in the 18th century, added to the treasure beliefs – although he was probably just an amateur archaeologist. Another old legend connects the same place with a fairy funeral; the grave being actually on the Mount.

The river was always an important focal point in the village, attracting many people who would not otherwise have visited Pulborough. In particular anglers come from miles around; young and old. The 'Seven Good Things of Sussex' include a Pulborough eel, which with a Chichester lobster and an Amberley trout, were considered the best of their kind. A recipe for cooking Pulborough eels has been sent to me by Evelyn Manvel.

> Two medium-sized eels
> 2 hard-boiled eggs
> Pickled pork (one third the weight of the eels).
> A little chopped parsley and onion
> Skin and bone the eels and cut into smallish
> pieces. Line a pudding basin with suet pastry,
> onion, the eggs cut up in four pieces and the pork.
> Fill the basin with stock made from the trimmings
> of the eels. Cover the suet crust and boil for two to
> three hours.

Pulborough must have had its witch, although no actual record of her seems to have survived. When a house was being renovated, the workmen discovered under the hearth a bottle containing about 200 pins. The commonly held belief was that if a number of pins became hot, they would prick the heart of a witch who was suspected of casting a spell upon someone in the house.

Pulborough folk seemed to have been rather a superstitious lot in days gone by. A swarm of bees on a dead tree was believed to fortell a death. A Pulborough lady who was expecting a baby, saw such a swarm and declared that it was a token sent to warn her that she would die in her confinement. Sadly this happened, much to the surprise of the doctor, but not of the father or the local nurse.

Nowadays we hear of moves to permit more Sunday opening by shops, but early in the 19th century there were strong attempts in Pulborough to cut down on the number of shops open on the Sabbath. The difficulty was that the farmers, who were the major employers, did not pay their workmen until late on Saturdays, and so their wives had to do their weekly shopping the next day. The anti-Sunday trading faction was

Pulborough Parish Church

successful, and from 14th February 1841 many shops closed on Sundays, following a promise by the farmers to pay out at 12 o'clock on Saturdays.

Unlike so many Sussex villages, Pulborough still has its railway station, with a number of residents using it each day to commute to London. When the railway was being built in 1859, the navvies lodged with the villagers. The beer-house keepers found themselves in trouble with the law, when they kept too generous hours in order to satisfy the thirst of the railway workers. There was one of the all too common fatal accidents, when one navvy who had been drinking fell asleep on the line, and was run over and killed by an engine bringing material for the continuation of the work.

Pycombe 🦢

If Pycombe had no other claim to fame than its shepherd's crook, it would still be an important Sussex village. Old shepherds claimed that they could tell where a particular crook had been made. Certainly this was true as far as the Pycombe crook (or 'sheep-hooke' as it was once called) was concerned.

One of the old crook makers at Pycombe was a Mr Berry, who worked at the forge from about 1820 to 1855. A later blacksmith was Mr Charles Mitchell, who made crooks for around sixty years.

It was Mr Berry who seems to have originated the particular Pycombe style, although he is said to have kept his methods of manufacture a secret. People in the know say that the best crooks were those made from old gun barrels. The sticks would be ash or hazel. The end of the crook, which is curled to avoid becoming a sharp point, is called the 'guide'. The guide on a Pycombe crook is always longer than on other crooks. Now old Pycombe hooks are collectors' items, and are found mainly in museums.

The Bishop of Lewes had a pastoral staff which consisted of a Pycombe crook on a hazel stick, made by Mr Charles Mitchell. Mr Mitchell's work became well known around the world, and he used to receive orders from as far away as New Zealand.

Mr Mitchell was once described as resembling a small lively

gnome. When Juliet Pannett drew his portrait in 1932, he said joyfully 'Wal, my wife wouldn't reckernise that!' When she asked him why not, he danced up and down with glee as he replied 'Cos she'm bin dead this twenty year'.

In more recent times the Pycombe forge has featured in a piece of revived folk-lore. A local character played the part of St. Clement (the patron saint of Sussex blacksmiths). There was also a witch, the Chanctonbury Ring Morris Men, and as the central part of the ceremony the 'firing of the anvil'.

In Pycombe's small church is something else metallic, of great interest; the 12th century drum-shaped font made of lead. The metal was cut flat and bent, and there is only the one seam. Tradition says that in the Civil War, the Puritan troops hunted out lead fonts to make bullets, and the Pycombe churchgoers whitewashed theirs, to disguise it. The action of the Puritans would help to explain why there are so few lead fonts in Sussex.

Arthur Beckett in the *The Spirit of the Downs* (1909) tells the story of Mr Hollingdale of Pycombe who lived in the 17th century. When the plague (probably cholera) came to the village, he built himself a cave about a mile away, thinking to escape, Unfortunately he came back too soon; and was buried in the churchyard.

Roffey

Originally known as Roughheath, Roughway or Roughey – there were also other spellings – this main-road village to the north of Horsham was apparently very aptly named. William Cobbett in his *Rural Rides* has this to say about the area in 1823:

'From Worth you come to Crawley along some pretty good land; you then turn to the left and go two miles along the road from the Wen (his name for London) to Brighton; then you turn to the right and go over six of the worst miles in England, which miles terminate but a few hundred yards before you enter Horsham......it was a bare heath with here and there, in the better parts of it, some scrubby birch. It has been in part planted with fir trees, which are as ugly as the heath was; and, in short, it is the most villanous tract......'

and much more in similar vein.

Anyone who has criticised Roffey in more recent times, would do well to reflect on how much worse it had been. Roffey once had a slightly workworn air about it; in my own youth I sometimes heard it referred to as 'Red Roffey', which I took to be a comment on some of its inhabitants' political leanings. But it has its own folklore and legends. The last Toll Gate House in the area was near Roffey's Star Inn. When the gate was in regular use, it was held to be responsible for bad weather: 'Someone has left the Star Gate open again' was sure to be the cry when the winds began to blow.

One of my childhood joys was to freewheel on my cycle all the way from the Star at Roffey to Horsham Carfax. I was told that the slope was such that the front step of the Star was exactly level with the tip of St. Mark's church steeple in North Street, Horsham. I didn't require proof, I was quite certain it was so!

Undoubtedly Roffey's nicest legend concerns its church, All Saints, which was consecrated on All Saints Day, November 1st, 1878. At the time the builders still had to finish off some of their work, and the scaffolding was still in position. A wild swan flew into one of the scaffold poles, dropping dead at the foot of the tower. The strange part of this tale is that the crest of the local Martyn family was a swan rising out of a crown; and it was Mrs. Cecil Martyn who had paid for the church to be built, also providing the ground. The incident was deemed to be a good omen, and the unfortunate bird's feathers were incorporated into the altar frontal. When they eventually disintegrated, the remnants were used on a canopy for processions.

The Roffey War Memorial takes the form of a Calvary, a crucifix of oak and teak, on the left of the pathway to the church door. It was dedicated by the Bishop of Chichester on October 4th 1919. In 1971 a yew tree was felled as part of a tidying up operation, and the Calvary was accidentally knocked over. The cross and base were damaged, but thankfully the figure of Christ was unharmed. The crucifix was fully restored, and re-dedicated on October 31st 1971, the yew tree being replaced by a rose bed.

At the original dedication of the War Memorial, buglers from Roffey Camp nearby sounded the last post and reveille. The camp had housed several different groups of soldiers during the First World War, the Kensingston 22nd Fusiliers, Canadians from Prince Edward Island, and later Portuguese. One day the latter mutinied against their officers – the officers hid themselves and sent for the local Catholic priest. In the meantime the Territorials from Crowborough were called. When they arrived the Portuguese climbed trees, but later said they would be good, came down from the trees and were duly sent to France.

The Officers' Mess remained, and became the home of the late John Rayner, a talented composer, who has yet to receive the recognition that would seem to be his due. Eleven of his songs have been published by Galliard as a collection, and included are some with Sussex connections, such as a setting of Hilaire Belloc's *West Sussex Drinking Song*.

Today Roffey is quieter and tidier than in the past. A relief road has taken a lot of traffic from the main road, and a new parade of shops near a new Star Inn supports the older shops in providing for the needs of the new housing estates.

Rogate 🌿

A small place with quite a lot of history – even if only of the 'villagey' kind. This is well wooded country; locally grown timber was an important commodity as far back as the 16th century, with wood being needed by the iron masters for the charcoal kilns, and the shipbuilders for the 'hearts of oak.'

Smugglers were busy in this area, and a local path is still known as Galley's Grove – named after William Galley, a customs officer who was murdered in 1748 and buried here by one of these gangs. The murderers were later apprehended and, after trial, executed.

To pass on to more pleasant matters: the church of St. Bartholomew was restored in 1875, but inside still retains several older things of interest, including a 14th century coffin stone and a 500 year old holy water stoup.

There were a number of old charities in the village. William

Wilkinson's charity of £2.0s.0d. yearly, derived from rent, was distributed to poor people on St. Thomas's Day. Mr John Souter left in trust the sum of £200, the interest being given annually to widows and orphans at the discretion of the vicar and churchwardens. Miss Simpson's charity consisted of the interest from £100 applied yearly to the upkeep of the churchyard, and the interest from £500 for the benefit of the parish.

Rogate had its own fair, said to go back as far as 1290. Originally a cattle fair, it later took on a more general character as the markets in neighbouring towns took over the regular sales of farm beasts. In September 1855 a Sussex newspaper reported that on the morning of fair day, a regular train of gypsies with their 'truck' put in an appearance, and there were few things missing from the make-up of a village fair; except Punch and Judy who were absent that year.

As well as the church band, there was also the village band, making its rounds at Christmas, and being rewarded with liquid refreshment in the process. Perhaps that is why on one occasion they are said to have serenaded a haystack, waiting for a welcoming light which failed to appear. Another village amusement was quoits, a game once very popular in Sussex. Here it was played with heavy iron rings.

For those who enjoyed themselves well but unwisely, or transgressed in some other way, there were the village stocks, which it seems lingered longer here than in some other places. They were finally put to rest by two villagers armed with pick-axes, spades and a cross-cut saw. For this the onlookers rewarded them with cheers, and even better, several gallons of beer.

There was published a few years ago a small booklet on St. Bartholomew's Church and Parish; anonymous and undated, but nevertheless full of fascinating village history.

Rudgwick 🦢

Called 'Rudgick' or 'Ridgick' by the older residents, it was also known in bygone days as 'The place where they sell fat pigs on Sundays.'

The single track railway line from Horsham to Guildford meandered in pre-Beeching days through some delightful Sussex and Surrey countryside, with little steam trains puffing between country stations still looking completely Victorian; many with beautifully kept gardens. The ingenious system of 'staffs' ensured that no train entered one section of track while it was occupied by another. I have many memories both happy and otherwise of this singular line, such as watching chickens on the tracks when a train was chuffing away quietly in one of the stations, or waiting on a freezing morning to be rescued by a diesel when one of the engines nearing the end of its life had given up the struggle. The last station just before the line entered Surrey was Rudgwick, it was said that here the porter called out 'Rudgwick' to the occupants of the First Class carriages, and 'Ridgick' to those in the Third.

Perhaps because of its nearness to Surrey, there seems to have been some rivalry between Ewhurst (in Surrey) and Rudgwick (in Sussex). At one time a traditional fight tok place each Whit Monday between 'The Kaffirs' of Coneyhurst Hill (in Ewhurst parish) and 'The Diamond-Topped Roundheads' of Rudgwick. The first name was evidently a corruption of Cavaliers, and it is interesting to conjecture on the origin of this annual event. It always took place at the Donkey Inn at Cranleigh; and on this one day of the year only.

In 1980 Rudgwick County Primary School celebrated its centenary, and one day in that year all the pupils and teachers dressed in Victorian clothes. The school was open to visitors, and an old style classroom was set up, with ancient desks which had been discovered in a storeroom, and with the teacher using an old fashioned blackboard. A special booklet to mark the event was produced, and the school also held a fair to pay for the cost of the celebrations.

Perhaps when the school was new some of the pupils may have recited this old rhyme, evidently part of a game:

'Warnham Once,
Rusper twice,
Rudgick three times over....'

Another folk rhyme which mentions the village, went like this:

'Rudgick for riches,
Green (Wisborough Green) for poors,
Billingshurst for pretty girls,
Horsham for whores.'

For the Queen's Silver Jubilee in 1977, a booklet compiled by
Barry Porthen was *Rudgwick's Celebrations*. It gives an
excellent idea of how one Sussex village marked the occasion
with a special church service, sporting events, a procession,
barn dance, fete and concert. Much detail is included, and there
are also several photographs. Local historians of the future will
be very grateful for such a record.

Rusper 🦞

I should not have favourites in a book of this kind, but if pressed
I must confess that Rusper would be high on my list. Many
years ago a newspaper described it as 'a village that has just
stood still', and despite a few additions, such a description
would not be too inappropriate even today.

To return to more solid matters. The interesting church of
St. Mary Magdalene has a large and impressive tower. Inside
are the royal arms of George I, and a number of old brasses.
Buried in the churchyard are the bones of some of the
Benedictine nuns from the Priory which existed until the 16th
century. The last part of the building was demolished in 1781,
and in 1840 when some additions were being made to the house
occupying the ancient site, several graves were discovered,
believed to be those of the Prioress and some of the sisters.
There were also a number of relics, including a beautiful
enamelled chalice, a small gold crucifix, a rosary, a gold ring, a
silver brooch and several pewter cups.

In the 19th century, Rusper church had a curate, Thomas
Smith, for eighteen years. He kept a pocket book in which he
recorded details of the village and its inhabitants. In 1821 there
were 69 houses with 89 families, comprising 487 men, women
and children. If each family occupied one house, that left 20
families unaccounted for! Just under 100 men were at work,
two thirds of them in agriculture. Some of his comments were a

little critical. Of one of the houses he wrote 'the house is the resort of young men – for the purpose of playing at cards and eating tarts and fruit.'

Horsham cobbler, Henry Burstow was one of the local singers who sang to the folk song collector Lucy Etheldred Broadwood (1858-1929), who lived at Lyne, near Rusper. There is an alabaster memorial to her on the west wall of the church, by Thomas J. Clapperton. She is also commemorated today by the Broadwood Morris Men, who dance regularly in Rusper and other Sussex villages, and who perform the Rusper mummers' play each Boxing Day.

Lucy Broadwood was described by Ralph Vaughan Williams as 'the greatest English folk song scholar'. Frank Howes wrote of her, 'Lucy Broadwood was one of those maiden aunts of independent means who in late Victorian times accomplished so much work of social value....' Her uncle, the Rev. John Broadwood, the squire-parson of Lyne, died in 1864, and evidently inspired his niece with his pioneer folk song collection of 1843, *Old English songs as now sung by the peasantry of the weald of Surrey and Sussex* (The full title is even longer). Only three copies of this privately printed collection are known, but it was undoubtedly a milestone in English folk song collecting.

Rusper has now, perhaps a little reluctantly, joined the rest of us in the 20th century – at least most of the time. But sometimes, there are moments when one is unsure. For instance in 1982 a gypsy woman who had been ordered to remove her caravan from a lane in the village pronounced a curse upon the three magistrates as she was led out of the court!

Rustington ✣

In 1835, Thomas Horsfield had this to say about Rustington:–

> 'The chief produce is corn. The method of tillage is what is termed three courses, i.e. sown with wheat every third year. The fuel is coal, brought to Little Hampton from the collieries in the north of England by sea.....The population of the parish in 1801 was 261; in 1831 not more than 365.'

When I stayed with my grandmother in Littlehampton in the 1920s and 30s, I remember Rustington as a real countrified village. Now I suppose one must refer to it as a small town, with an excellent shopping centre. Once it had its own windmill standing close to the sea, but in spite of a sea-wall meant to protect it, it was finally swallowed up by the tides. As may be expected, smuggling went on here, and even as late as 1860 forty-five tubs of smuggled spirits were washed ashore. It seems that the smugglers had intended to run the cargo to the west side of Littlehampton, but they were surprised in the attempt and sank the tubs, hoping for a later opportunity to reclaim them. The strong current washed the cargo ashore, where they were discovered by the coastguard and taken to the custom house at Arundel.

The composer Hubert Parry lived at Rustington for thirty-seven years, and it was here he wrote the music for the world famous anthem *Jerusalem*.

In recent times another composer lived at Rustington, Peter Nightingale, who as well as having written a vast amount of music, founded an orchestra for his musical family and their friends in 1974. From this nucleus grew the Young People's Light Orchestra which now gives many concerts of classical, light, folk and pop-style music – always for charity. The ages of the members of the orchestra range from 7 to 25 years, and many start playing almost from their first introduction, as all the parts for the lower grades are tailor-made. There is now also a choir, the Orchestra Singers. The musicians and singers have travelled many hundreds of miles giving concerts, both in England and abroad. So far they have visited France, The United States, Canada and Holland, and in 1984 they plan a round trip to Europe, which will take in France, Germany, Luxembourg and Belgium.

I am always interested to hear about modern events, which may become annual customs with their own traditions in the years ahead. Rustington has a Boxing Day Pram Race, which raises cash for charity. The competitors dress in fancy costume, ranging from Punch and Judy to Tom and Jerry.

Salvington 🖎

The Parish Register for 1584 records that 'John, the son of John Selden the minstrell, was baptised'. This was John Selden, the eminent scholar and literary figure. It was said of him that he was of such stupendous learning in all kinds and all languages, that it could be thought that he had never spent an hour but in reading and writing. The cottage, now demolished, where he was born was then known as 'Lacies', and on the lintel of the door he was supposed at ten years old to have composed and carved an inscription, which has had several translations – one of which is:

'Thou'rt welcome, honest friend, walk in, make free,
Thief get thee gone; my doors are closed to thee.'

About a mile from the village stands High Salvington Mill, the last surviving example of a 'post and socket' mill in Sussex. This is a mill which is suspended on a post, and may be turned by means of a tailpiece. It is so perfectly balanced that it was said the miller's daughter could turn it unaided.

The central post was once thought to be an oak tree, trimmed and used where it stood, but certain authorities have doubts about this. It is also thought to be the first windmill in England to have been insured against fire.

The mill was last worked in the 1914-18 war, but between the wars was kept in good order and open to the public. The store room was turned into a tea room, and this helped to make it a very popular place with visitors. Many picture postcards of the mill as it was at this period may still be found. Since the last war, the mill's condition has been the cause of concern, but it is now receiving care from several groups, and it seems that its future well-being is assured.

Selsey 🖎

Once known as Seal's Island (and even Holy Island, for reasons which will become obvious), this was once a true island entirely surrounded by sea, but is now a peninsula. Selsey Bill is its extreme point, and is in fact the most southerly portion of Sussex. The erosion along this part of the coast has lost Selsey about half a mile of its land since Domesday.

Arthur Beckett in his *Song of the Sussex Men,* that rollicking poem that should really be sung, has told the legend of St. Wilfred and Sussex, in four compact lines:

> 'Saint Wilfred sailed to Sussex, an' he come to Selsey Bill,
> An' there he built a liddle church upon a liddle hill:
> He taught the starving pagans how to net fish from the sea,
> An' then he them converted all to Christianitee.'

St. Wilfred's first church in Sussex has been called 'the cathedral under the sea', and everyone seems agreed that after he taught the starving Selsey folk how to fish, they were so impressed that they agreed to build a grand edifice to the glory of God. But that church now lies under the waves, and local folklore adds that at low tides the bells can still be heard. Another church replaced the sunken cathedral, in the 13th century, and the chancel of that still remains as a chapel at Church Norton. In the 19th century the church of St. Peter's was built in the village, utilising some of the stone from the earlier building.

Also below the sea, there lies what was, 400 years ago, an extensive deer park, and the stretch of water covering it is still known to the fishermen as 'the park'. In the reign of Henry VIII, some poachers broke into the park, and proceeded to poach the deer. This so enraged Bishop Rede, that he pronounced excommunication on them, ordering every church in the diocese to carry this out by 'bell, book and candle', the priests declaring 'so shall the light of the offenders be extinguished forever'. They didn't waste much sympathy on poachers at that time!

Fishing was long the Selsey men's main occupation. Cockles, prawns, lobsters and crabs were once extensively sought out here, and oysters were taken in large quantities. A Selsey

161

Cockle was one of the traditional 'Seven Good things of Sussex', along with the Chichester Lobster and the Arundel Mullet. Bones of an immense size were washed ashore in the 18th century, and even during the 19th fishermen dredging for oysters would bring similar bones to the surface, along with huge tree trunks and fossil shells.

Of course fishing was always a hazardous occupation along this coast. In 1881 the Selsey Coastguard spotted a light burning some miles out to sea, and assuming it to be a distress signal, launched their boat. Sure enough the light was on a fishing boat which had been caught in bad weather. Supplies were almost exhausted, and the crew of five men and a boy were reduced to burning their own clothes to try and attract attention. They were brought ashore, and dried out in the Fisherman's Joy inn.

But not every fisherman's day was that bad. Every year there was 'Crabber's Day', a traditional day-out for the fishing families; which after being allowed to lapse, was revived in 1979.

Selsey ought to be popular with treasure seekers. A pot containing 1,000 Roman coins was found there, also on two occasions golden circlets have been discovered on the shore.

For a small place, Selsey has much to write about. There was 'the Hundred of Manhood and Selsey Tramway' (later 'the West Sussex Railway'). It was described by the *Chichester Observer* in 1909 as 'the noisiest and most rickety railway in England'. It earned itself several nicknames; 'Clicket Click or Bumpity Bump', 'the Blackberry Line', 'the Selsey Bumper' and 'the Hedgerow Railway'. The latter name was because the line hugged the hedges, to avoid the owners having to purchase additional land.

The main purpose of the little railway was to link Selsey to Chichester; it was but seven miles long, and was completed in 1897. In its most prosperous days it carried over 80,000 passengers a year, but it passed into history in 1935.

One of the most intriguing residents of Selsey was Colin Pullinger who lived there during the last century. He was born in 1815, his father being a carpenter. After trying several occupations, he opened a factory in the High Street, and had trade cards printed which read as follows:

162

Colin Pullinger. Selsey near Chichester.
Contractor, Inventor, Fisherman and Mechanic,
following the various trades of a builder,
carpenter, joiner, sawyer, undertaker, turner,
cooper, painter, glazier, wooden pump maker,
paper hanger, bell hanger, sign painter, boat
builder, clock cleaner, repairer of clocks and keys
fitted. Repairer of umbrellas and parasols.
Mender of china and glass. Copying clerk, letter
writer, accounts, teacher of navigation. Grocer,
baker, farmer. Assessor and collector of taxes,
surveyor, house agent, engineer, land measurer,
assistant overseer, Clerk at the parish vestry
meetings, Clerk to the Selsey Police, Clerk to the
Selsey Sparrow Club.

Shermanbury ✍

This is truly Roadmender Country, for it was here at Mock Bridge House that Michael Fairless wrote her famous and many times reprinted book *The Roadmender.*

Michael Fairless was actually Margaret Fairless Barber, born in 1869 at Castle Hill, Rastrick, in the West Riding of Yorkshire. In her teens she became afflicted by a spinal weakness, but in spite of this she trained as a nurse in a children's hopital. Later she had recurring and painful attacks of illness, and when she became too ill to carry on other activities she began to write. When she was unable to manage the physical effort required, she dictated. While living on the Chelsea Embankment, she conceived a longing for the green hills of Sussex, and once there she seemed completely content, although her health did not improve. She died on 24th August 1901 in her 33rd year, and was buried at Ashurst. She wrote about Sussex in a very spiritual way, and her books have struck answering chords from a great many readers all over the world.

Shermanbury was unfortunate in one of its visitors in the 18th century. Dr Burton of Oxford came to the village in 1751 to see his mother, who had married the rector. Of the local squires he had this to say:

'You should observe that the farmers of the better sort are considered here as squires. These men, however, boast of honourable lineage, and, like oaks among shrubs, look down upon the rural vulgar. You would be surprised at the uncouth dignity of these men, and their palpably ludicrous pride.... being illiterate they shun the lettered; being sots, the sober. Their whole attention is given to their cattle and everything else fat, their own intellect not excepted.'

Shipley

If you visit Shipley, probably the first building you will notice is King's Mill, one of the tallest windmills in Sussex, totalling nearly 100 feet from the ground to the tip of the sails. It cost £2,500 to erect in 1879, a large figure for that time. It was built by the Horsham millwrights and engineers, Grist and Steele, who always seemed to me to be very well named. Mr Grist was apparently a very fat gentleman, as I can remember one of my aunts quoting an old local saying 'as fat as old Grist', when speaking of someone particularly large.

In 1906 the well-known writer Hilaire Belloc purchased the mill and King's Land, the house adjoining, which had previously been the village store. Born in France in 1870, with an English mother and a French father, he spent much of his childhood at Slindon, so Sussex can truly be considered his adopted county. Belloc's habit when returning to Shipley from one of his many trips was to doff his large black hat to the mill, known as 'Mrs Shipley'. He wrote over 100 works, but liked to be considered a country farmer rather than a writer. He was a well-known figure locally; at West Grinstead where he worshipped at the Roman Catholic church, and in Horsham. He is still remembered for his rather flamboyant appearance – which far from resenting, most local people viewed with pride.

Shipley mill ceased working in 1926, when Belloc asked that it should be closed (after all, he was the landlord) as the mill traffic past his study window was becoming a distraction. The mill is now well cared for, and is open regularly to the public,

Shipley Windmill

with Shipley folk very much in evidence, showing visitors around, providing teas and doing all that is necessary. A plaque over the door referring to Hilaire Belloc says he 'garnered a harvest of wisdom and sympathy for young and old'.

Shipley was a very industrious place. There were the woods, with all the attendant activities including the iron forges working night and day. Horseshoes were manufactured here, and bolts for crossbows. There were also several quarries in the area.

In spite of all this apparent prosperity, Shipley had its workhouse, which incidentally enjoyed a very bad reputation. In 1830 the population of Shipley was 1,180, with 113 families receiving relief and 46 paupers in the workhouse. Among the numerous rules relating to the inmates was one that ordered 'that any female being in the family way shall be degraded by wearing a party coloured or workhouse dress'. In a report dated 1st August 1836 by the Medical Officer of Health, it was stated 'there was not a healthy person in the house except the master and a portion of his family.... in three months there were eight deaths, mostly from fever.... the water supply was not pure and the supply was short....' Local people, used as they were to bad conditions, were sufficiently aroused by these circumstances to attempt to alter them, particularly where children were involved. One man, a shoemaker named Mills of Horsham, who had been forced against his will to send three grandchildren to the workhouse, was particularly worried when he heard that the children had been moved from Warnham to Shipley. He walked to Shipley to see for himself, did not like what he saw and removed his children, first giving the workhouse master the benefit of his indignation. For his honest wrath he was subsequently committed for trial at the Sussex Quarter Sessions, and although he apologised for his remarks, he was sentenced to six weeks hard labour. When he returned to Horsham after serving his sentence, he was received as a hero by the townsfolk, but this didn't alter the conditions at the ill-famed Shipley workhouse.

Another chapter in Shipley's history concerned the notorious Shipley Gang, a band of criminals who terrorised the inhabitants early in the 19th century. Highway robbery, housebreaking and sheep stealing were all included in their activities, and all these were carried out quite ruthlessly. James Rapley, who liked to be known as 'Robin Hood' was the leader, although his moral code was very unlike that of the legendary outlaw. Finally after a virtual reign of terror, most of the gang were captured, and James Rapley committed suicide in his prison cell. A new gang replaced the older one, but with little of the ruthlessness or spirit of the original. It confined its activities entirely to poaching, carrying this on in an almost respectable way. They had their regular customers, and would even carry addressed labels with them, to tie straight on to poached items, so that they could be despatched to their destinations without delay.

Sidlesham ✍️

On one side of Pagham Harbour, Sidlesham once had a busy quay with ships loading for France. Now the harbour is useless for large vessels, but has become a haven for wild life.

Another prosperous piece of Sidlesham's past was the mill worked by the power of the tides. One writer in 1804 called it 'inferior to none in the kingdom'. The boast was that it could grind a whole load of wheat in an hour.

One of Sidlesham's three old inns is the Crab and Lobster. There is a legend that there was fight between Cavaliers and Roundheads on the quayside. All the Cavaliers were killed, except for one who escaped into the inn. Later he was discovered by the Roundheads and was quickly sent to join his dead comrades.

In the 1930s a brave attempt was made to set up small holdings in this rich agricultural land. Each unemployed family was provided with three acres, and some livestock.

Singleton ✍️

Called Silletone in the Domesday Book, later Sengleton, and finally Singleton; the name means thicket or a bundle of wood.

The church of St. John the Evangelist is full of interesting things – some old stained glass, a gallery, monuments and tombs, ancient graffiti and examples of Petworth and Sussex marble. A monument to Thomas Johnson (1744) a famous huntsman of the Charlton Hunt, has this rhyme beneath it:

'Here Johnson lies. What Hunter can deny
Old, honest Tom the Tribute of a sigh
Deaf is that ear, which caught the op'ning Sound
Dumb is that Tongue, which chear'd the Hills
around

Unpleasing Truth – Death hunts us from our
Birth
In view; and Men, like Foxes, take to Earth.'

The first Women's Institute in England was at Singleton in
1915. The movement was started in Canada, and quickly
spread to this country. The first English President of a village
W.I. was Mrs Leveson-Gower; President of Singleton W.I.

In earlier times Singleton was not the law abiding village it is
today. Smugglers flourished, with the old Drovers Inn as their

Charcoal Burner's Hut, Singleton

headquarters, where there were useful cellars and secret passages. There was a gallows on the Trundle, where Tapner, the leader of a band of ruthless smugglers, was hung in chains after a smuggling raid in 1747. The gallows remained until 1791 when it was truck by lightning. There are also tales of highwaymen plying their trade in this area.

Nowadays Singleton is really two villages. The ancient one I have been describing, and the Weald and Downland Open Air Museum, which was opened to the public in May 1971. Its main purpose is to rescue good examples of vernacular architecture, such as farmhouses, small village and town houses, and shops. The museum is growing all the time, and is fast becoming a small town of interesting old buildings of different periods, together with examples of the trades, crafts and traditional life of the south eastern part of England.

There is a useful small guide to the church and village, anonymous but well written. Ian Serraillier has compiled a most entertaining book *All Change at Singleton* (1979), consisting mainly of old photographs with explanatory captions; but what photographs! I would say this is one of the best collections of old pictures devoted to one Sussex district, and the author deserves great credit for the way the book has been arranged and written up. For instance there is Tom Reeves the carrier, with his horse and cart. Ian Serraillier has written 'Tom Reeves, carrier, lived at Pricklows, and the cart was kept in a wooden shed (now demolished) which backed up against the house. His brother Alf was often the driver, as Tom was busy with other things; he owned a timber cart, employed two men on haulage, worked in the woods and sold bunts (small faggots). A big card with R on it, placed in a front window, was the customer's signal to the carrier to call. His charge for an order was 2d to 6d. For collecting a box of 15 dozen eggs, delivering it in Chichester and returning it empty, the charge was 3d. For 6d he sometimes took a passenger to Chichester, saving him the long trek to Singleton station. To rest the horse he left it in the yard at The Fountain in South Street. Delivery and collection at the shops took much of the rest of the time, and it was often 9 pm. before he was home again'. There is much more of similarly detailed information accompanying most of the photographs.

from 1886-7 for Singleton Stores, kept by W. Miles. As well as such varied stock as boots and shoes, ready-made clothes, hosiery, drapery and haberdashery, wedding cakes, new laid eggs, wood, coal and sheep coops; there were also 'The Celebrated Novelty Sausages'. Further details of the latter are lacking, but one is left with a mental picture of all kinds of possibilities, including bangers that really went bang.

The aforementioned Trundle is the hill close to Singleton, which has a number of very persistent traditions attached to it. The most common is the belief that a Golden Calf is buried there. In Parish's *Dictionary of Sussex Dialect* (1875) there is an explanation of the Sussex countryman's habit of using 'He' instead of the 'Devil', when the evil one was being discussed. He went on to relate 'In the Downs there's a golden calf buried; people know very well where it is – I could show you the place any day. Then why don't they dig it up? Oh, it is not allowed; 'He' would not let them. Has anyone ever tried? Oh, yes, but it's never there when you look, 'He' moves it away'. This is taken to refer to the Trundle.

Another belief is that it is gold or some other treasure that is buried on the hill, left behind by the Vikings. Anyone unwise enough to attempt to dig it up is stopped either by a storm, or by a ghostly calf left to guard it.

Slaugham 🦢

Like several other Sussex villages, Slaugham is not pronounced as it is spelled, but as Slaffam – a typical Sussex ploy to confuse the 'furriners'.

This delightful spot is surprisingly quiet, considering its closeness to the London-Brighton main road. The church of St. Mary looks out onto the green, where the Lord of the Manor paid for the telephone wires to be hidden underground, and the telephone box was painted white.

The church and churchyard have much of interest, including a small sculpture by a local parson, and the tomb of Nelson's younger sister, Catherine Matcham, who lived nearby with her husband and eleven children. The attractive lines of the church with its 13th century tower can now be seen to advantage, but some old photos I have show that at one time it was largely obscured by the White Horse pub, which was removed in 1922.

Not far away was a once locally famous medicinal spring. The site was well known in the latter part of the 17th century when some ladies of the local family of Covert had a bowl carved out of sandstone, into which the water welled up via a hole in the base. Once this little healing spring was known as 'My Ladies' Bowl', and a Horsham man with a dog-cart and another man from Brighton, came regularly to take supplies of the water back with them, which presumably they sold.

Once Slaugham Place housed a family of seventy persons. Now the Elizabethan house is in ruins, and only the staircase is preserved in Lewes Town Hall. The ruins have a melancholy beauty about them, and once when I saw them covered in snow, they looked positively unearthly.

Local legends exist regarding underground tunnels and chambers which are said to lie beneath Slaugham Park. It has been stated that after a fall of snow, the air in the tunnels, which is of a higher temperature than the frozen ground, prevents the snow from remaining and a pattern of shapes and continuous lengths can be seen. The tunnels are supposed to lead to a vault in the church, and into the wood on the further side of the road between Slaugham and Staplefield. There are also stories of a ghost of a Grey Lady and of Roman soldiers.

Slindon ᘓᕗ

> 'Though Slindon is a little spot,
> Its fame has travelled far;
> There's scarce another place, I wot,
> Wherein such wonders are begot,
> As Slindon's wonders are.'

The start of a poem written by W. Victor Cook, sets the scene so well for a look at a place full of wonders – starting with the parish church of St. Mary, which among many other interesting things has the only wooden effigy in a Sussex church. It is probably of Sir Anthony St. Leger (1539), a 5 foot figure in armour. Not too many Sussex villages have Roman Catholic

171

churches, but Slindon has St. Richard's, built as long ago as 1865. Inside is a tiny monument commemorating Antony, Earl of Newburgh (1814) by a Danish sculptor, Bertel Thorwaldsen.

Slindon Fair on St. Swithin's Day, July 15th, was also the day of the annual cricket match, which started promptly at 11 o'clock when the clock on the stable block of Slindon House struck the hours. In the evening the annual village fights took place, when Slindonians settled their grievances for another year.

Nore Folly, on the hill half a mile from the village, is often the subject of speculation regarding its origin. The usual story is that a bricklayer named Samuel Refoy, unable to find work, was asked by the Countess of Newbury if he could build her a copy of an arch shown in a print she had brought home from Italy. She was so pleased with the result, that he was made estate bricklayer at Slindon House. The room inside, used for shooting parties, was added later.

Slindon has a number of ghost stories; the most persistent being a legend of a riderless horse seen at different times on Slindon Down. Horses owned by local people are also supposed to have refused to pass the spot where the ghostly white horse was seen.

Ghosts and smugglers often seem to go together, and Slindon was undoubtedly a place full of the latter. One of the best known local stories is about 'Godiva of Slindon', the grisly details of which are as follows. Betsy Thorpe was a local girl, the sweetheart of Will Garland, a Customs Officer. Ben Tapner was the leader of one of the most desperate gangs of smugglers in the area. One day Garland had an opportunity to capture one of Tapner's gang, who was shot in the arm in the struggle. When Tapner heard of the arrest, he swore vengeance, and it was not long before the gang captured the Customs man when he was on his beat. They gagged and bound him, and took him away as their prisoner. When Betsy heard what had happened, she boldly presented herself at the cottage of Ben Tapner, and enquired what was to happen to Will. She was told that his punishment was to be whipped naked across Slindon Common, and without a thought the girl offered herself in place of her lover. Tapner, brute that he was agreed – and so it was done, but poor brave Betsy died of the ordeal, and later her Will was shot by the smugglers.

There was a woodland craft carried out at Slindon, which was a little unusual. In the beech woods above the village, they once made wooden wedges for use in ship building. The beechwood wedges used to be stacked in their thousands, before being transported to their destination. Wood unsuitable for wedges was fashioned into floats for fishing nets.

Slindon House has been mentioned several times. A one time butler at the big house, Mr. William Pearse, was a natural artist, and many of his pictures of local scenes remain in the homes of older residents. He is buried in the churchyard of St. Mary's, where he worshipped regularly.

Slinfold 🐚

A very pretty village with some fine Georgian houses. The Roman Stane Street passes through the parish, and the main village road is called simply 'The Street'. At Roman Gate on the main Guildford-Horsham road there was a toll house, kept for a time by a deaf old lady who was regularly terrorised by the local children on their way to Slinfold school.

Nairn and Pevsner are very enthusiastic about Slinfold, describing everything as 'mellow', and giving as their opinion that the best individual house in the village is the modern 'Brickwood' (1961) in the centre. St. Peter's church (1861) they described as 'proud and uncompromising, but not unsympathetic'.

This was a particularly industrious place, with the remains of the iron industry still in evidence in the locality of Roman Woods. (Furnace Farm, and the position of an old furnace pond and a hammer pond shown on maps, are excellent evidence.) Other traditional industries were hoop making (for barrels), charcoal burning in the woods, a tanyard, brickworks, a basket factory and the timber yard, which even had its own private siding from the single track rail line running from Horsham to Guildford. On Whit Tuesday there was an annual Pedlar's Fair. At the fair in 1797, there was an incident caused by a group of

173

drunken soldiers from Horsham Barracks, who tore down stalls, took possession of the pub, and finally broke all the mugs and crockery in the place. On their way back to Horsham, they stole a flitch of bacon from the pub at Broadbridge Heath. No doubt the authorities dealt with them in a suitably severe manner.

One of the most important of the local industries was the quarrying of Horsham Stone, in several places. This stone was once carried by water from near Slinfold to the sea, and thence to many different destinations. Although now exhausted, the quarries at one time supplied huge pieces of Horsham Stone for use on roofs and pavements all over Sussex, and elsewhere.

A comparatively modern custom was carried out annually at Slinfold school, earlier in this century, when the children wore sprays of Lily of the Valley on Ascension Day, signifying a 'ladder to heaven'.

Small Dole 🌿

The intriguingly named tiny village near Henfield, is the home of the Sussex Trust for Nature Conservation, which has its headquarters at Woods Mill.

A water mill has been on the site since the time of the Conqueror. It was a working mill until 1927, becoming a tea garden in the 1930s. In 1950 it was bought by Dr. J.N. Douglas-Smith, whose family gave it to the Trust in 1966. The mill has four storeys, and much of the machinery can be seen, as well as many other interesting exhibits. Outside there is a Nature Trail, also 'The Ancestors' – carved statues of knights in armour. Their origin is not known, although they are not of great age; but little boys love them.

An interesting description of the mill as it was nearly thirty years ago, appears in the *Sussex County Magazine,* July 1956.

As well as a good place to spend an afternoon, Woods Mill may encourage you to support the Sussex Trust, by becoming a member.

Sompting ✦

Sompting was described in the mid 19th century as 'pleasantly situated and marked by rural simplicity'. The population at that time was 519. By 1901 it had increased to 679, and the area was said to be very suitable for market gardens, with the chief crops being wheat, oats, mangold wurzels, turnips and clover.

The great treasure of the village is the church of St. Mary famed for its Saxon tower with its Rhenish Helm – the only one of its kind in the country. It is mentioned in Domesday, and the church has a history of over 900 years. Roman remains have several times been found in the area. In 1971 there was a find of rare Samian pottery, and there have also been several discoveries of early jewellery, and a rare bronze urn.

One of the imaginary place names of Sussex folklore is the Sompting Treacle Mine, and at nearby Worthing a saying is that anyone who is particularly lazy works at that place. In *The Folklore of Sussex* (1973) Jacqueline Simpson credits 'Jimmy Smuggles', an imaginary local character, with the invention of the treacle mine. Jimmy also invented many other wonders, such as a porridge quarry, bottled moonlight, handkerchiefs for weeping willows and a device for lifting holes over walls. Such local humour, in this case well-chronicled by Alfred Longley of Worthing, is priceless, and should be noted down whenever possible, before it completely disappears in this age of videos and computers.

Sompting was fortunate in its local characters. Its strong man, Alfred Blaker, was credited with lifting a large pig single-handed into a cart, after it became loose. In 1870 he was said to have almost knocked over Lancing signal box, when he accidentally leant on it when rather well oiled.

But undoubtedly, Sompting's greatest character was Edward John Trelawney (1792-1881) who dwelt here for the last twelve years of his life. Starting his adventurous life as a boy in the navy, he soon distinguished himself by his remarkable courage. He went on to live a life of tremendous enthusiasms and dashing deeds, later on becoming a friend of Byron and Shelley. After a life full of wild activity, he found peace in Sompting, where he called the birds with a bell and gave the children Turkish delight. He died in 1881, under blue Sussex skies, although his body was taken to Rome to rest beside that of his friend Shelley.

South Stoke 🌿

The church dedicated to St. Leonard still has much of the original 11th century building. As a correspondent to the *West Sussex Gazette* pointed out in January 1984, the church has no electricity, but every year there is a candle-lit carol service on Christmas Eve, with people coming from near and far. The service is followed by the serving of hot soup for all who desire it.

Southwater 🌿

The Southwater bypass was completed several months ahead of schedule, as the County Council continued to tell motorists by means of a large sign, long after the new road was open and in daily use.

The new road was not the only change in recent years. In 1983 the big chimney of Southwater brickworks, which had been a local landmark since 1890, was demolished – marking the first step in the creation of a 42 acre country park. The brickworks were closed two years earlier, when the clay ran out; and the owners Redland Bricks had the bright idea of turning the blowing-up of the chimney into a lottery prize, with the proceeds going to local charities.

It was in the clay pits of the brick works that fossilized bones of the Iguandon were discovered in 1928 and again in 1940. Could these have had some connection with the persistent dragon legends encountered in this part of Sussex?

The last Southwater windmill was in the quaintly named Cripplegate Lane, but this went the way of many Sussex windmills and was burnt down in the early hours of May 25th 1914, in spite of the attempts by the Horsham Fire Brigade to save it.

Although it is on the main Worthing Road, Southwater has always retained its village identity and country manners. A local farmer was credited with the following quintuple negative early in this century: 'Dunt know nobody who arnt got no pig taters they dont want to sell, do ye?'

One lady told me of her grandfather who was a carter on a Southwater farm. At 9.00pm each night he went back to the farm to 'rack the horses'. Occasionally he found them in a sweaty and disturbed state, which he blamed on ghosts in the stables. He firmly believed in this, and so did his grandchildren when he told them about it. This reminded me very much of similar stories from the coastal parts of Sussex, when fairies were considered responsible for horses being found in a similar state, although perhaps it should have been smugglers who received the blame.

In the 17th and 18th centuries Sussex produced some notable diarists. By the 19th, the fashion for keeping detailed diaries had largely passed, although a Southwater farmer was an exception to the rule. He was Henry J. Smith, who compiled a virtual history of the village from 1837 to 1907. Originally privately printed early in this century, it was made available again in 1977. From Mr. Smith's notes we learn that Southwater had two annual fairs, one on Easter Monday and another on July 8th. There was a gingerbread stall run by Dame Rayley of Shipley, whose trade was leech-catcher. She caught them in a pond (Leech Pool) in St. Leonard's Forest and supplied them to local doctors. In 1860 the building of the railway was begun, and the usual run of accidents is recorded. In 1863 a large balloon holding nine people landed in a field at the Misses Dendy's Pond Farm, and in 1894 the diary states simply 'Czar of Russia died' and 'George Smart died'. The journal closed when the farmer was turned 80.

Staplefield

A large green with a church dedicated to St. Mark, built in 1847. The clock on the church dates from 1877, and was apparently installed to help the local children to get to school in good time.

Unusual for a small village, Staplefield also has a Roman Catholic church, which was originally a Baptist chapel. The church was dedicated to Our Lady of Fatima in 1966.

But in spite of two churches, Staplefield was not always law abiding. In 1777 four soldiers attacked a larger number of smugglers on the common; but the latter were the victors and gave the soldiers a severe beating.

In a previous book I printed a photograph of two shepherds of Staplefield, taken on May Day 1918. The shepherds are wearing smocks and carrying crooks, and as well as a dog they have two sheep, both decorated with May garlands – a custom usually confined to children. The shepherd on the left with the beard is Henry Etherton who lived at Nymans Cottages, Tanyard Lane, Staplefield, and who was employed by the Messel family at Nymans, Handcross. The second shepherd is a Mr. Selby who also lived at Nymans Cottages.

Once quoits were very popular in Sussex, and many village pubs had their own teams. Now the only place where the game is still played – as far as I know – is Staplefield, at the Victory pub, each Boxing Day.

Stedham

A pretty village with an old six-arch bridge over the Rother. A Sussex guide from the beginning of the century mentions a reading room with a library of 150 volumes 'intended for the benefit of the villagers who pay one penny a week'. It also speaks of the famous churchyard yew 'supposed to be over 900 years old'. The church of St. James had seats for a congregation of 250, of which '114 are free'.

Stedham had its witch, who could halt a carter's wagon, until the spell was broken by whipping the wheel. (It was more usual to break a witch's spell by means of something made of iron).

Mavis Budd has written several books about life in Sussex earlier in this century. The setting for her books is around Stedham and Trotton, and although full of wisdom and nostalgia, they are also extremely funny. The ones most often met with are *Fit for a Duchess* (1970) and *Dust to Dust* (1966). She writes with affection of her grandparents, and her grandmother's lotions and remedies form the basis of another of her books called *So Beautiful* (1981). Most of the recipes are full of good sense, even probably the cure for hiccoughs, which is 'Say 'welcome stranger' over and over again, until the hiccoughs cease.'

Stopham ✺

The church of St. Mary, a few cottages and the famous bridge – considered by all who see it as one of the finest and most attractive of medieval bridges in the country. It was built in 1309 and rebuilt in 1403. Six of the arches are original, but the seventh in the centre was raised in 1822 to permit the passage of barges. The bridge is preserved, but is frequently under repair due to the amount of traffic which uses it. Those who care for such things worry about the possibility of a second bridge beside it, to carry heavy traffic. Logically a splendid idea, but aesthetically disastrous.

The little church is filled with memorials of the Bartelott family. One of the former rectors was Thomas Newcombe, the author of a long poem in twelve books called *The Last Judgement*.

This most beautiful part of Sussex once saw oxen ploughing regularly on its farms. A Sussex newspaper for October 10th 1796 reported a ploughing match near Stopham Bridge between oxen in yokes and oxen in harness, and also oxen and horses. But of course eventually both were superseded by mechanisation.

Stoughton ✺

The church of St. Mary is on the hillside north of the village. Nairn and Pevsner describe it as 'plain outside and impressively rich inside'. Arthur Stanley Cooke in *Off the Beaten Track in Sussex* is even more outspoken. While admitting that the church is 'lofty and spacious within' he described the outside as of an 'ugliness almost unredeemed'. It has been conjectured that one of its priests must have loved it very much, as he still frequents it. There is a story of a ghostly monk or priest who has several times been seen moving about within, particularly near the altar. Once he was seen outside, coming out of a door which had been blocked up. It was said that this door had formerly been used by the priest after the communion. Near the inside of the door there is an ancient piscina.

A more solid figure of the past was George Brown, nicknamed Brown of Brighton, who was born in Stoughton in 1783. He was a fast bowler, and his arm was reputed to be as thick as another man's thigh. He could throw a ball 137 yards, and was credited with having thrown a ball right through a coat, killing a dog on the other side. Somehow, I am not surprised to hear that he sired seventeen children. A solid man without doubt!

The most famous feature of the area is Kingley Vale, the nature reserve owned by the Sussex Trust for Nature Conservation. Sometimes called 'The Great Yew Forest' a book by this name, written by Richard Williamson (1978) will satisfy all who wish to read in depth of the natural history of this fascinating place.

Yew trees are said to have been growing here for 2,000 years, and this is the largest forest of them in Europe. Battles were fought here between Britons and Danes, and legends and ghost stories abound. There are four large barrows known as The King's Graves or The Devil's Humps. Legend has it that if you walk round them the magical seven times, the Devil will come out. (Similar Devil stories exist elsewhere in Sussex.) Danes and Druids are said to haunt the dark and wooded vale, and even the trees themselves are said to assume other shapes at will. The place is so solemn and sombre that one would be surprised if there were no such stories.

Sullington 🌿

The sexton at St. Mary's Sullington, for 35 years was often heard to say that he would like to die doing the job he loved. One Sunday morning in 1941 he opened up the church, sat down in a pew with the key in front of him, and was found there by the organist a little later – his duty done.

This is one of the interesting pieces of local history within a little book by R.L. Hayward *Yesterday in Sullington*. Like so many Sussex villages, Sullington has been well served by a local chronicler.

In an alcove in the tower of the church there is an effigy of a knight, thought to be the oldest stone monument in Sussex. The figure is in chain mail, the left arm bearing a shield and the left hand a sword. The right hand has been broken off and the feet are missing. The knight is thought to be a De Covert, possibly Sir William who was lord of the manor in the 13th century, or one of his relatives. The effigy originally lay in the north aisle but was moved to its present position in 1873.

The church is so near to the Manor Farm house, that approaching it one is inclined to think that the two are both within the farm yard. The huge tithe barn is 115 feet long, built mainly of large beams and tarred weather boarding. The date 1685, which is said to be when it was restored rather than built, can be clearly seen on one of the beams. The inside, when it is not being used for storing sacks of wheat, makes a perfect setting for a country barn dance, holding band, caller and a hundred or so dancers with ease.

The novelist A.J. Cronin wrote his famous story *The Citadel* when he lived in a house in Sullington. He and his wife spent months painting and decorating the old rectory after they had discovered it by accident, and decided that this was where they must live. From the garden he could see Chanctonbury Ring, and the quietness and peace must have been exactly what he needed for his writing.

Sullington Warren, nearly 30 acres of it, is a stretch of heathland where the gorse blooms in the spring and the heather in the autumn. It was acquired by the National Trust, with much financial help from local people.

Truly this is a beautiful piece of Sussex, which may partly explain why the Rev. George Palmer and his son Rev. Henry Palmer between them filled the rectorship of the parish for a century. This is what Canon Palmer wrote in 1862:

'I know of no more beautiful view than that one
from our downs just at this time of the year, on a
day like this: a delicate blue haze in the distance

just not obscuring the sea, Isle of Wight and Reigate Downs; in the foreground, waving breadths of wheat.'

Tangmere ✺

If Tangmere has any folklore, it must relate to the Battle of Britain, as the place is best known as the site of one of the famous World War II aerodromes. The air force base was built in the early 1930s, but the history of the village goes back a good deal longer, and the 12th and 13th century church of St. Andrew has several things of interest. One of these is a mysterious sculpture above one of the windows, which it has been conjectured may have come from the lost Selsey Cathedral. The subject is uncertain, but one suggestion is that it is the head of St. John the Baptist as presented on a plate to Salome.

When I visited Tangmere I found the old Officers' Mess being put to good use as a community hall. The pub also has air force connections and bears the very appropriate name of The Bader Arms, after the World War II flying ace Sir Douglas Bader who was stationed at the RAF station. The Bader Arms was opened in 1981 by Sir Douglas, who in characteristic Bader style pronounced the sign 'bloody awful'. In 1983 a new pub sign painted by Michael Pearson, working from a portrait of Sir Douglas Bader, was unveiled by Lady Bader, widow of the legless pilot. She commented that she thought the new sign would meet with the approval of her late husband. The ceremony was followed by a flypast of RAF planes and a display of aerobatics.

Tarring ✺

Most people now refer to it simply as Tarring, although more correctly it should be West Tarring or Tarring Peverell, to distinguish it from East Tarring or Tarring Neville, in East Sussex.

Villages which lie close to a large town often become

182

swallowed up by the larger place. Tarring has retained its individual character mainly by reason of its attractive curving High Street. Here are the three timber-framed cottages of Parsonage Row, owned by the Sussex Archaeological Society. For an all too short period, there was a museum of Sussex folklore, but this no longer exists.

The Parish Hall was originally the Palace of the Archbishop of Canterbury. Tarring's best known piece of folklore concerns St. Thomas a'Becket who often stayed in the village. The orchard of fig trees nearby is said to consist entirely of trees descended from one planted by Becket about 1162. In fact one particular tree is reputed to be the very one planted by the Archbishop's own hand, although the majority of the orchard trees date from 1745.

As is evident by the fig trees, the climate of this part of Sussex is very gentle, hence the large number of market gardens in the vicinity of Worthing.

The church of St. Andrew is large, with a tall spire – one of the few unofficial buildings in Sussex allowed to fly the White Ensign. The font is modern, replacing an older one which for some unexplained reason was taken to Australia and installed in Melbourne Cathedral.

The church possessed the right of sanctuary. When John le Messier who had stabbed Simon de Goringe, took advantage of this right and subsequently escaped, the village was fined in consequence.

The church was fortunate in retaining its parish records covering a period of about 200 years. Included in the churchwarden's accounts are the charges concerned with the Church Ales, including the cost of minstrels, a play, bells for the morris dancers, a bagpipe player, the hire of a cauldron and of course much food and drink. Earlier these festivities must have been held in the church itself, but later a church house was provided.

Thakeham 🦋

Because of its remoteness, this charming village was once dubbed 'the last place God made'. No doubt merely jealousy on the part of one of its less attractive neighbours.

A trifle more complimentary was the rhyme which started 'Thakeham Boys are Bulldogs'.

One of the best known songs in Sussex, *Buttercup Joe* also commemorates the place in this fashion:

> 'Now I be a rustic sort of chap,
> My Mother lives o'er Thakeham.'

However, it should be admitted that sometimes some other village is substituted – but this is the version I sing!

In the 19th century wagers involving the consumption of vast quantities of food were not uncommon. Can it have been that this was the only way certain members of the less fortunate classes could ever hope to eat their fill? In 1800 a journeyman

Church of St Mary, Thakeham

blacksmith of Thakeham undertook for a small bet to eat a pound of new butter, with bread in proportion, and to drink a quart of beer, all in the space of thirty minutes. He made no difficulty of it, and seemed ready for a second attempt.

Inside the church of St. Mary, there was once a musician's gallery, where, presumably at different periods, a band of players and a church barrel organ were said to have provided the accompaniment to the hymns.

Two old inhabitants of Thakeham have been given a facelift, and changed their way of life. They are two small locomotives employed on a 2 foot gauge railway at Thakeham Tile Works until November 1980, when they were handed over to the Chalk Pits Industrial Museum at Amberley. They took their ¼ mile long track and two waggons with them. The little work-horses were Hudson-Hunslet diesel locomotives dating from the 2nd World War. They were used to carry block making materials, a job which is now being done by a conveyor belt.

This was the last working 24 inch gauge railway in Sussex, all that remained of a once large layout. The locomotives have been named Thakeham 3 and Thakeham 4, and new name plates were made for them by members of the Steyning Grammar School's metal-work department.

Three Bridges 🐝

Many rail travellers know Three Bridges as the rather large station which they use when changing from the Portsmouth to the Brighton line. Before the railway, Three Bridges was a very small village in the shadow of the slightly larger Crawley. Now that the latter is a large new town, Three Bridges is one of the several villages that have become part of the new conurbation. Although there are rail lines across separate bridges over the main road, the name predates the railway and refers to much earlier bridges. The railway brought much new employment to the village, and some modest prosperity. Although it is now very much part of Crawley, there is still a little of the character of the old village left, including several pubs and the lines of Victorian houses originally occupied by the railway workers.

There are also some of the original residents, who view with

185

some dismay the exceptional changes which have taken place since Crawley became one the of post-war new towns. One man who refuses to be worried by the changes is Mr Jim Laker of Three Bridges who has lived in this area all his life. In 1914 his family moved from Three Bridges to Worth Lodge Farm, and he grew up as a real country boy with many memories of farming life at the very end of the period before total mechanisation and modernisation. Later he moved back to Three Bridges, and during his retirement he has taken a tremendous interest in the changes which have taken place around his homes over the past seventy years. He has collected a vast array of old picture postcards and photographs of the area, which he has put on public show several times. He has also written two books – *Down Memory Lane* in 1979 and *Yesterday's Child* in 1981. These personal memories of a relatively small community are extremely valuable, and we must be very grateful to men like Mr Laker who have used their leisure time to reach back into the past in this way.

Tillington

About a mile from Petworth, this village boasts a landmark which is unique in Sussex. It is the Corona at the top of the tower of the church of All Hallows. It is formed of flying buttresses at the four corners, meeting in a finial and forming a Scots crown. Built in 1807, it is not only the only one of its kind in Sussex, but one of very few in England. The designer's name has not come down to us with any certainty, although a nice tradition credits it to Turner who had been trained as an architect. A local artist Chris Rolfe used it on a Christmas card, and it can also be seen very plainly on the cover of the Oxford University Press reprint of Hugh de Selincourt's famous Sussex story *The Cricket Match*. Tillingfold is the name he gave his fictitious village, although the actual place that provided his inspiration was Storrington.

The village is unashamedly old fashioned, and between it and Petworth there is that very old fashioned thing, a haunted lane. Said to be troubled by a headless horse, it also once had parts which real horses almost refused to cross.

The Sussex Garland of 1851, described the lane at that time in this way: 'The lane is scooped out of rocks by the winding of the deluge, it would seem, by the mighty workings of the water, and canopied over by hazels and sycamores interlacing each other from their opposite banks, and the banks studded with more variety of, and more beautiful flowers than even Sussex lanes are usually decked with......'

Tinsley Green ✺

The little hamlet of Tinsley Green lies in the shadow of the giant Gatwick Airport, and close to the main railway line. Apart from a few nice old houses, the only building that most people notice is the spacious Greyhound Inn, in the forecourt of which the famed Tinsley Green marble championship takes place each Good Friday. Once called Marble Day in Sussex, this was the day of the year when Sussex people (adults and children) played marbles in the streets, on the village greens and even in the churchyards. They also skipped, played bat-and-trap and planted their potatoes; but most of all they played marbles. After noon on Good Friday no marbles were supposed to be played until the following year. If they were, they could be snatched away and kept with a cry of 'Smugs' or a similar magical word.

Sam Spooner, who was born in 1861 was a marble champion in the 1890s and one of the first players at Tinsley Green when the games were organised into the championship we know today. According to Sam, marbles were first played at Tinsley Green in the reign of Queen Elizabeth; local lads played for the hand of a rosy-cheeked maid. They have been played in or around Tinsley Green ever since.

At Tinsley Green forty nine marbles are placed in the six foot ring (four marbles for each of the two team's six players; plus one). A line is made in the sand and the two captains then stand over the line and drop their tolleys (the shooting marble) from nose level. The tolley nearest the line wins and goes first. The initial shot is made from the edge of the ring. If a player shoots and stays in the ring without knocking a marble out, his tolley must stay in the ring until the player's next shot. If the tolley is knocked out before his next shot, the player is 'killed' and takes no further part in the game. If the player knocks a marble out of the ring and his tolley remains in, he can continue shooting until he misses. The winning team is the one with the most marbles, or over half the total number.

Trotton ✥

Trotton is very much in the border country between Midhurst and Petworth. It has been suggested that Trotton Bridge, first noted in the 14th century, which spans the western Rother, may have been built originally on stepping stones set into the bed of the river. It was built or perhaps rebuilt by Thomas Lord Camoys, who was also the builder of the church of St. George close by.

The church is famous for its brasses. The central tomb is 9 feet long, dated 1419, and is of Thomas de Camoys and his wife and son. Thomas was a baron during Richard II's reign and accompanied Henry V at Agincourt. His wife Elisabeth was the 'Gentle Kate' of Shakespeare's *Henry IV*. In the floor is the earliest church brass in England to show a lady. It is dated 1310 and is of Margaret de Camoys. Other Trotton men besides the baron may have been at Agincourt, as the village was noted for its archers and it has been conjectured that the grooves on the door jambs of the church were worn thus by archers sharpening their arrows.

The church was extensively restored in 1904, and a very interesting account of this restoration appears in the *Sussex County Magazine* for January 1956, written by H.M. Alderman who was a young apprentice at the time.

Before the restoration was finally completed, details of the rector, architect, builder and workmen were placed under the external boarding. A short summary of world events in 1904, such as the Russo-Japanese war, was also included. The whole of the restoration work cost less than £700.

The good old custom of an annual harvest supper was kept up at Trotton, and the 1883 feast hosted by Mr. Toop of Gatehouse Farm was reported in a Sussex newspaper of the

188

time: 'After sitting down to one of Mrs. Toop's best dinners; song, toast and sentiment went merrily round, whilst the health of the founder of the feast, and the mistress, were sung as lustily as we ever remember to have heard them before'.

It has been said that Sussex has three great poets – Otway, Collins and Shelley – although I wonder how many know much of the former. Thomas Otway was born at Trotton on August 22nd 1717, the only son of Humphrey Otway, curate of the village and afterwards rector of Woolbeding. Otway the poet died at 33, and is buried in St. Clement Danes, but a tablet to his memory is in Trotton church. One of the other two Sussex poets mentioned, Collins in his *Ode to Pity*, linked Otway's name with the Arun, or rather its tributary the Rother:

> 'Wild Arun, too, has heard thy strains,
> And echo, 'midst my native plains,
> Been soothed by Pity's lute.
> There first the wren thy myrtles shed,
> On gentlest Otway's infant head.'

Twineham 🐚

An old prophecy is supposed to promise that the good folk of Twineham will be the first to awaken at the end of the world. The author Thurston Hopkins disagreed. In *The Lure of Sussex* (1928) he wrote 'Slow inertia will keep the living inhabitants of Twineham from making a move until half the dead of the world have mobilised. To startle the village would constitute a miracle....' Even assuming him to be correct, why should not the residents of this delightfully quiet backwater remain in their blissfully quiescent state for as long as possible.

In the churchyard of the brick church of St. Peter, the local Quakers were once allocated a section to themselves – an early example of ecumenism. A commentator on the music inside the church early in the 19th century, had this to say 'The bandsmen and choirmen were of the peasant class; they assembled occasionally in each other's cottages for a practice. Some of them were quite unable to read, and had learnt the anthems from hearing them sung by others'. Canon Macdermott in his

Sussex Church Music in the Past (1922) spoke of the leader of the Twineham church choir in the last century, who could sing the whole of the psalms and many anthems entirely from memory.

All this sounds as if Twineham was an old fashioned sort of place, and perhaps it still is. Jacqueline Simpson, the Sussex folklorist, mentions that even as recently as 1952 a Twineham man carried out the traditional ritual of 'telling the bees' at a farm, when they had passed into the ownership of a new master and mistress. The bees which had been swarming, then settled down.

Here is a recipe for an oatmeal pudding enjoyed by the Stapley family of Hickstead Place:

> Of oats decorticated take two pound,
> And of new milk enough the same to dround;
> Of raisins of the sun, ston'd, ounces eight;
> Of currants, cleanly picked, and equal weight;
> Of suet, finely sliced, an ounce at least,
> And six eggs newly taken from the nest;
> Season this mixture well with salt and spice;
> And you may safely feed on it like farmers,
> For the receipt is learned Dr. Harmer's.

Two-Mile-Ash

This is a small hamlet near Southwater, which does not feature in many Sussex books or on maps. It has an inn known by the charming name of Bax Castle, although the local name at one time was The Donkey, as there was always a donkey tied up there. The name has given rise to the belief that it was connected in some way with the composer, Sir Arnold Bax, who lived in Sussex. However, there seems little doubt that this is a story without foundation, as several people who have knowledge of the area have pointed out that the pub has had its name since the 19th century, long before the famous composer was even born. It seems far more likely that the name came from a local weaver of home-spun linen who lived in the house.

Upper Beeding 🦜

There are two Beedings in West Sussex; Upper which is four miles inland from the sea at Shoreham, and Lower, four miles from Horsham. Oddly enough Upper Beeding is lower down on the bank of the Adur, and therefore could be considered lower than Lower Beeding. Just to add to the confusion, Upper Beeding is more often than not referred to as just 'Beeding'.

At the beginning of the nineteenth century the village was an important link in the system of toll roads, and the Beeding toll cottage was probably the last to close in Sussex. It can still be seen, at the Singleton open-air museum. Bramber is very near to Upper Beeding, but winter floods have been known to cut the two off from each other. The bridge probably replaced the old Roman ford across the estuary. When the future King Charles II was fleeing from the Roundheads, he was nearly captured by the soldiers guarding the bridge.

The church of St. Peter is thought to be on the site of a Saxon church built in the century following St. Wilfrid's introduction of Christianity into Sussex. After the Norman conquest a stone church replaced the earlier one, and the last major rebuilding took place in 1308. The church band once included that obsolete but aptly named instrument – the serpent. It was 7 feet 10 inches long, made of thin wood covered with leather and had four keys. A picture of the Upper Beeding serpent appears in Canon Macdermott's book *Sussex Church Music in the Past* (1922).

The Baptist Church had an interesting beginning. Early in this century a farmer from the West Country, Mr. T.D. Cross, came to Sussex with his wife, family of ten children, farm workers, horses and cattle. The family were Baptists, and as well as joining the nearest Baptist church which was at Shoreham, they started a Sunday School in their own kitchen at Beeding Court Farm. In 1913 a mission hall was built as the farm kitchen was unable to accommodate all who wanted to come. In 1959 the Beeding Mission became a fully-fledged Baptist church, and was followed by a new building in 1966.

In many Sussex towns and villages on December 21st – St. Thomas' Day – there once existed a very pleasant custom known as 'Gooding' when the poorer women went from house to house to beg a little something towards the Christmas festivities. They were seldom unrewarded, and widows in particular received generous treatment. Many of the donors kept to a regular routine of alms giving each year, and at Beeding the vicar sat at his study window doling out a silver coin to any old woman who cared to bring him a sprig of evergreens.

One of Upper Beeding's sons was a shepherd named Michael Blann, who was born in 1843, the fifth child of Edmund Blann, a sawyer, and his wife Mary. When only nine years old he began his career as a shepherd on the Downs above Beeding for the then useful sum of three shillings and sixpence a week. The family had a tradition of singing, and as Michael travelled to Findon, Lewes and other sheep fairs, he increased his own repertoire of songs. By 1867 he had begun to write down his favourite songs in a notebook, which can now be seen in Worthing Museum. As well as singing, he also played the tin whistle, a skill not uncommon among South Down shepherds. He performed at Harvest Suppers and local concerts, and although no stone marks his final resting place in Patching churchyard, a fitting memorial to him was published in 1979 – a fifty five page book *Shepherd of the Downs* by Colin Andrews. The book, published by Worthing Museum, included biographical notes on Michael and the songs from his notebook, set to suitable tunes.

Walberton

Walberton gained the award for the best kept large village in Sussex, so its neatness is no surprise. A handsome arch of oak was erected on the village green in 1937 to mark the reign of King George V and Queen Mary, and the coronation of King George VI and Queen Elizabeth. A few years ago the uprights were found to be unsafe, and after heroic fund raising efforts they were replaced by a local craftsman, who also recarved the lettering on the top beam of the arch.

The church of St. Mary was rather clumsily restored in 1903, but there is still much of interest including a stone font, and a stone coffin dug up in the churchyard in 1834.

In 1817 in a field within the parish, an unusual find was made by workmen who were making holes with a crowbar to erect sheep hurdles. Their bar met with resistance at about a depth of six inches, and a stone about 4 feet long and 20 inches wide was found to be the obstruction. Underneath was a chest 18 inches deep containing about 28 articles including basins, plates, jugs, saucers and a number of smooth pebble-like stones. What was described as the 'most beautiful object' was a flat bottomed square bottle in transparent sea-green glass, nearly full of calcined bones. At one end of the chest were two lamps and at the other a pair of small sandals. Except for the latter, all the articles were in perfect condition.

Not all Walberton farmers were so lucky. In 1880 one of them was complaining over the crop of flints on his fields, and was advised to try 'flint soup'. Sussex farmers were sometimes credited with the belief that stones really did grow on their fields, even when other crops would not.

On May Day a century ago in this village, as elsewhere in Sussex, the children carried flower garlands from house to house begging half-pennies and pennies. In 1881 one little girl was unlucky enough to lose all but one halfpenny out of her total takings of fourpence, when her father confiscated the larger share to spend on his 'bakker'.

My collection of old Sussex photographs was enlarged in 1982 when I was given the opportunity to have copies made of a small collection of pictures from early in the 20th century, all of Walberton and close by. Included was a photograph of the November 5th bonfire on the green surrounded by a group of children in dark suits and flat caps (the boys) and white aprons and long dresses (the girls). The only relatively modern photograph was from 1937, and showed a group of school children in the playground enjoying T.T. milk from Mr. Cox's Dairy, Slindon.

Warmingshurst 🦡

One of the truly great men of Sussex, William Penn, lived at Warminghurst for twenty-five years. Before settling there he went to Pennsylvania, and on his return thousands assembled to hear him speak. The religious intolerance of the time is aptly illustrated by the wording of a charge against Penn, soon after he had achieved world-wide recognition for his peaceful settlement with the American Indians. The long diatribe began in this fashion:-

> 'For as much as the Grand Jury at this present
> Sessions have presented William Penn of
> Warminghurst in this county of Sussex gent for
> being a factious and seditious person and that he
> doth frequently entertain and keepe unlawfull
> assemblyes and conventicules in his dwelling
> house at Warminghurst aforesayd at which
> conventicules there are usually assembled the
> number of one or two hundred unknown persons
> and sometimes more to the terror of the King's
> Liege people and in contempt of our sovereign
> Lord the King and of his lawes and thereupon they
> did humbly desire this Court that the sayd
> William Penn might finde Suretyes for the Peace
> and his good behaviour.'

And so on, with more much in the same, to us, rather ridiculous vein.

A later owner of the house where William Penn lived, is the subject of a very tidy ghost story. I describe it so, as unlike so many ghost stories it has a beginning, an end and a point. In December 1766, Mr John Butler left his home at Warminghurst for London, to take his seat in the House of Commons. The following morning his sister-in-law was startled to see his ghost walk through her bedroom. Later the steward of the estate told her that he had also seen the spirit of Mr Butler, in his office. On neither occasion did the ghost speak or reply when spoken to. During the afternoon Mr Butler's groom returned with the news that his master had suffered a fatal heart attack just about the time he had apparently appeared to Miss Browne and the steward. No will could be found, until it was remembered that Mr Butler sometimes kept papers in the room next to his sister-in-law's, where his ghost had been seen to go. After much searching there, it was discovered.

194

Warnham 🕮

'On Christmas Eve, 1846, I was standing with a
brother ringer, Wm. Norket, at the bottom of the
Bishopric; 'twas a clear frosty evening, with the
wind in the north, and as we stood we heard the six
Warnham bells ringing beautifully.'

So wrote Henry Burstow of Horsham in his locally published
Reminiscences. Warnham has been a bell-ringing village for a
long, long time, and the ringing-chamber of the church of St.
Margaret (originally St. Mary) offers a fascinating glimpse into
the past with the many notices and lists of old ringers around the
walls. There are now eight bells; two being added to Henry
Burstow's six in 1885.

In the churchyard can be seen the tombstone of Warnham's
grand old man, Michael Turner. The easily read inscription
ends:

> 'And when at last, his age had passed
> one hundred less eleven.
> With faithful cling to fiddle string,
> he sang himself to Heaven.'

Not entirely poet's licence, as Michael died at the age of 89 (in
1885) holding his beloved fiddle.

As well as being the village musician of his day – he played
both in church and for feasts and fairs – he was also Parish Clerk
and leader of the church choir. Something of a dandy it seems,
as a picture of him as a young man shows him wearing a tall hat
and shiny boots. Some memories of Michael were handed down
to me via the daughter of a Warnham man who was one of the
choirboys. 'He was a stern taskmaster and if any of the
choirboys misbehaved he would grab them by the scruff of the
neck and bang their heads together. Many times my head was
left spinning after an upset with old Michael'. The choir at this
period wore white smocks in church, and sat on the gravestones
in the churchyard before the service, smoking their clay pipes.

Warnham seems always to have been a busy village, with not

only bell ringers (handbells as well as church bells), but dramatic and choral societies, cricketers and today a Local Historical Society. The Village Hall must have provided the setting for much of this activity, and musicians remember with a certain rueful nostalgia the bathroom-like acoustics of the first hall built in 1892. The present-day hall is a beautiful building, perfect acoustically and in most other respects.

Not in the village, but within the parish of Warnham is Field Place, the birthplace of the poet Percy Bysshe Shelley. Born in 1792, until the age of ten he was educated in the village. Later his chosen paths were to take him far from the simple surroundings of his youth.

Warnham Court c 1908

Almost without a doubt the best known name in Warnham is that of the Lucas family. A lady born in the village in the closing years of the last century told me how 'old Mr Lucas' looked after the workers on the Warnham Court Estate. At Christmas all the women had a pound of tea and a red flannel petticoat.

The Warnham mill and the large millpond are nearer to Horsham than the centre of the village, and although skaters no longer risk their lives in the winter months on the thin ice, the younger element still fish regularly from the bridge – just as my father did. My own Warnham memories are of fishing in the clay pits of Warnham's brickyards, on the north side of the

196

village. Just as many older Sussex houses are roofed with Horsham stone slabs, so many of the more modern ones are built of the locally renowned Warnham bricks.

Warningcamp 🦡

Not surprisingly one of the suggested derivations of the name of this small village was that it had once been an army camp, from which warning of an attack could be sent to Arundel Castle; although this all sounds just a little too plausible.

The 18th century seems to have been a popular time for hermits and recluses. Warningcamp had Charles Verral, son of Richard Verral of the White Hart at Lewes, who lived here from about 1770 to 1790, and was known as the Hermit of Warningcamp. He dwelt in a habitation he had built himself on the site of an old chapel, and which he called 'New Jerusalem'.

In 1863 the Sussex newspapers were reporting a monster snake having been sighted several times in the vicinity of this village. It was stated to be 8 feet in length with a girth greatly exceeding what would be proportionate. An organised crusade against the life of the unfortunate creature was being contemplated.

Rather more attractive creatures were the dancing bears, which could be seen around the countryside with their handlers in the 19th century – although possibly just as repellent to many people, but for quite different reasons. Their life on the road, being made to perform to the will of their human companion, must have been anything but easy. A correspondent of the *West Sussex Gazette* in 1961 recalled how in 1892 on the Warningcamp Road, he and his father saw four or five bears, including one very large one, taking their Sunday rest beneath an overgrown hedge. The bears' owners had met at this remote spot to spend a little relaxation together. The bears were led by a chain fixed to their muzzle, and they spent the nights in any convenient barn or outhouse, when a farmer could be persuaded to allow it. One lady told me how as a young girl she spent a very frightened night, because she knew her father had agreed to one of these bear men putting his charge in a shed beneath her bedroom window.

Washington 🌿

The most famous landmark of the South Downs, Chanctonbury Ring, overlooks the village of Washington. The beech trees on the summit were planted on what was once a bare hill, by Charles Goring of Wiston Park, as a boy in 1760, but these were sadly decimated by the great gale of 1987.

There are several local folk stories connected with Chanctonbury Ring. The most persistent is that if you run round it seven times at midnight (some say it must be backwards) the Devil will appear and reward you with a bowl of soup (or milk). Sometimes the belief is attached to Midsummer Eve, the night when fairies are supposed to be abroad on the Ring. There was a Roman temple here, and folklorists believe that these old beliefs involving running in a circle, go back to the time when ritual round dances were carried on here. To spend a night on Chanctonbury Ring is said to be an eerie experience, and many otherwise level-headed folk have detected a feeling of great unease for no apparent reason.

Chanctonbury Farm was the location of a great find of Saxon coins in 1866. It consisted of an urn containing some 3,000 pennies, supposed to have been buried just before the Battle of Hastings. The coins were at first dispersed locally, and sold from hand to hand for quite small amounts. Eventually the Treasury rounded up most of them, and antiquarians found that the coins represented some fifty different mints, including Chichester, Lewes, Steyning and Hastings. Before the find, a tradition of a local treasure had existed for many years. The spot was supposed to have been haunted by the ghost of an old man with a white beard, who always appeared to be searching for something. In spite of the treasure being recovered, the field was still considered as haunted even up to more modern times.

The grand old man of Washington is Mr. Herbert Goatcher, retired market gardener, who lived in the family home overlooking Goatcher's Nurseries. When I met him, he had collected a delightful series of old photographs of the village, and had been writing his own memories, which he hoped eventually would be published. He also showed me many bygones such as a handmade candle lantern, fashioned by the local blacksmith and containing Sussex glass, and a beautifully made miniature barrel, an exact replica of a full sized one, made by a local cooper. This had been used by his grandfather to take cider or small beer with him into the fields. There were also working and Sunday smocks which had been owned by his grandfather, still in perfect condition, very heavy and well able to withstand wind and a good deal of wet. He allowed me to try them on, and I found a smock to be exceedingly warm and comfortable, just as I had always expected. His grandfather wore one for his work in the nursery, and another to go to church on Sundays. Mr. Goatcher said that the last people to wear smocks in the village were the shepherds.

Washington had several industries. There was a limeworks run by the Floate family, and a large sandpit, both of which helped to supply Worthing with building materials. There was also a timber yard with two saw pits, and a small brickworks, remembered today by Brickyard Pond where the clay was dug.

The Washington windmill, 'Rock Mill', was erected in 1827, and eventually became the home of the composer John Ireland. He first discovered Sussex in the 1920s and he said 'much of my music has been inspired by Sussex and its ancient past'. *Amberley Wild Brooks* is one of his best known works, not only inspired by the county, but with one of its most lovely areas as its title. In 1980 the mill, now without its sails, was offered for sale consisting of an octagonal sitting room, dining room, study, kitchen, breakfast room, five bedrooms, two bathrooms, circular observatory, utility room and sun room.

West Chiltington 🥬

Lord Ponsonby said 'If West Chiltington Church was in Italy, people would make pilgrimages to it'. Like the village itself, the church of St. Mary is a showpiece, and even if no one actually makes pilgrimages to it, it must receive plenty of visitors. Inside the church are a number of mural paintings uncovered in 1882, some almost as old as the building itself. A unique feature of the church is the exceptionally long hagioscope or squint, from the south aisle to the chancel. This was probably because at one time there would have been a bell rope hanging in the south aisle, and an altar server would need to see the priest to know the exact moment to ring the bell at the elevation and consecration of the sacred host.

For a long time the dedication of the church was not known, but a will dated 1541 was discovered in which John Sayrle directed that his body should be 'buried in the churchyard of our Lady of Chiltington'.

West Chiltington windmill was a smock mill of which the cap only and not the body revolved. It was originally built in the 18th century in Monckmead, and was dismantled and rebuilt in its present position. It last worked in the 1920s, and has now been converted into a house. In 1963 it was offered for sale with the accommodation comprising a main reception room, drawing room, dining room, four bedrooms, three bathrooms, kitchen and balcony.

The name Smock Alley has caused quite an amount of controversy from time to time. Many different explanations for the name have been offered. Smoke from the local mists, flowers called Ladies' Smocks; or a laundress who washed smocks and hung them out to dry. There was an ale house here which had a reputation for smuggling. It was said to have had a false window sill where contraband was hidden.

Old Dame Jackson was the local witch, claiming to be capable of curing earache, toothache, bellyache and rheumatism. For all these complaints she used oil taken from adders, for which she paid one penny each.

West Dean ✣

There are two West Deans in Sussex, one in East Sussex, and this one in West, on a lane running parallel to the road from Chichester to Midhurst. The church of St. Andrew suffered a bad fire in 1934, but has been rebuilt since. The three east windows are a memorial to a gentleman killed by elephants.

Mrs. Charlotte Latham (*Some West Sussex Superstitions.* 1878) has one of the many Sussex witch stories concerning the use of a bottle of pins, as an antidote to a charm. A friend of Mrs. Latham, Mrs. Paxton of West Dean, told her how she saw upon a cottage hearth, a quart glass jar filled with pins. Upon enquiring why they were there, she was informed that it was a

200

charm recommended by a 'wise woman' to combat the daughter's falling-fits, which it was believed had been caused by witchcraft. When the pins became red hot, they were supposed to prick the heart of the witch who was responsible for the girl's affliction.

Westergate ✣

Westergate, the twin of Eastergate, is in the popular market-garden area of West Sussex. It has a poignant legend of an 18th century married couple who left the village to live for a time in tropical climes. The wife returned some time before her husband, and in due course gave birth to a child who was black. The woman was terrified, and tried by constant bathing and scrubbing of the baby to render it white, but all to no avail. Her husband's reactions when he returned are not recorded, but the episode was handed on to posterity by a sign on the local pub; once the house where the couple lived. One side shows a black boy in a bath with his mother scrubbing him, the other shows the woman surveying her useless labour with consternation writ large on her face. The name of the pub The Labour in Vain sums up the story quite neatly. For a time the sign was considered unsuitable and was removed, but in 1927, The New Inn, as it had been re-christened, reverted to its original name, and a new version of the old sign went up. I sincerely hope that the present day race-relations people will have enough sense of humour to allow the pub to keep its sign.

Gerard Young in his book *The Cottage in the Fields* (1945) when dealing with Sussex ghosts he had known, described a house in Westergate as the most haunted building in his part of the county. In one room the brickwork bulged out in a slight curve, and tradition stated that it was here that a girl's murdered lover was incarcerated. Some people are supposed to have felt what they took to be a heavy blow on the head when they entered this room, sufficient to knock them unconscious. Many residents of the house complained of the sound of a body being dragged along the floor. In the same house was a door which never failed to bang, even on completely still days, and servants felt a cold wind sweep down a passage. By taking inside and outside measurements, it has been ascertained that a secret room exists, although the entrance to it has never been discovered.

West Grinstead ❧

West Grinstead's church dedicated to St. George, stands a long way away from any houses, close by the river Adur. One of the most noticeable things in the church is the way that the names of local farms have been lettered on the back of the pews. The named seats were occupied by the men, the seating at the back being for the women and children. There are a number of large monuments, including one to Captain Powlett, whose unquiet ghost is said to haunt St. Leonard's Forest, although no one seems to know why. Like most country churchyards, this one had secular uses; fairs and markets were held, and archery was practised, even on Sundays. In 1399 William Wyling was shot through the leg with an arrow in the churchyard.

In the grounds of West Grinstead Park, there is an oak tree under which Pope is said to have written most of *The Rape of the Lock.* Another tree, this one a maple, is supposed to have the gift of bestowing long life on children who have been passed through its branches. When a rumour spread in the 19th century that the tree was to be cut down, petitions were presented that it might be spared.

Smugglers operated here in the 18th century, and tradition states that one of them had a fine horse which he used to dope with beefsteak soaked in brandy, which he tied to the horses's bit. With this stimulent the horse was supposed to go like wildfire and to do sixty miles in a day. This smuggler called Downer, and his partner Nailard, subsequently made a fortune smuggling and then drank themselves to death.

In more modern times an ancient custom was being revived at the Tabby Cat pub when the local Morris Men wassailed the apple trees. This was first done in 1981 and the old trees in the pub garden yielded such a magnificent crop that the landlord has gladly consented to the same ritual being carried out since.

The Roman Catholic church of Our Lady of consolation, was attended by Hilaire Belloc during the time he lived at Shipley, and his grave and memorial may be seen next to the Tower door. Local people still remember his unmistakable figure in a long black coat, sometimes with the bulge of a bottle of sherry as a gift for the priest. Occasionally he would be accompanied by his friend G.K. Chesterton. They always sat in the same pew in the church, and one lady told me how as a girl she was shoo-ed out with the familiar black coat, when she inadvertently sat in the wrong seat.

Next to the church is the priest's house, which incorporates an earlier chapel used by the Sussex Catholic family of Carylls, who owned West Grinstead Park. Under the floor in 1925 were found a pewter travelling chalice c. 1430, and another of about 1600. These must have been used by priests who spent their lives hiding from the authorities, and saying mass for the faithful whenever an opportunity presented itself. The chapel may now be visited easily by pilgrims, although once entry to it must have been through a narrow aperture. The ceiling was raised over the altar, so that the priest could raise the sacred host as high as his arms would allow, the small congregation crying out 'Hold! Sir Priest, hold!'

West Hoathly 🦢

Sometimes called West Ho-ly by older residents; a village full of charm and beauty, standing on a high hill. The church of St Margaret of Antioch is the main point of interest, with a unique churchyard consisting of six terraces, each built up with a retaining wall. In springtime this hillside is blaze of colour, and a verse on a stone gives some idea of the view:

> 'Friend looking out on this wide Sussex view,
> Know they who rest here had also loved it too.
> Pray then like them to sleep life's labour past,
> In your remembered fields at home at last.'

Opposite the church is the beautiful Priest House. Over 500 years old; since 1935 it has been in the care of the Sussex Archaeological Society, and open to the public as a folk museum. Inside there is a delightful collection of bygones,

The Priest House, West Hoathly

kitchenware, samplers, needlework, Victorian dolls and the like. When I last visited it, the lady custodian went out of her way to make my visit pleasant. When she knew that I was researching old Sussex games, she delved into her memory for an occasion in West Hoathly many years before, when a game had been played with a really huge ball; but unfortunately that was all she could recall.

Gravetye Manor House was once the home of one of the local iron-masters, Richard Infield. When the iron industry departed from Sussex, the house stood empty and was used by the smugglers. These gentlemen are said to have murdered a village girl who discovered their cache, and she was left to die alone in the deserted house. Later the property became famous for the garden created by William Robinson. Born in 1838, in Ireland, he rose from garden boy to foreman in Ballykilcannon. In 1861 he left Ireland for the Royal Botanic Society's gardens in Regents Park. He prospered, educated himself, and became the gardening correspondent of the *Times,* and founder of several gardening journals. In 1884 he was able to afford to buy Gravetye Manor, living there until his death in 1935, aged 97.

He never married, and was sometimes called the greatest English gardener.

In 1947 'rough music' was revived at West Hoathly. The victim was a man who complained to the police about the noise made by some young people in the village. In retaliation, the noise became 'rough music' made by pots, kettles, horns, bells and drums; continuing for the regulation three nights. When asked why they were doing it, the reply was 'It is our right!' Although the custom had not been carried out within living memory, it was still considered a 'right'.

A very complete history of West Hoathly *The Story of a Forest Village* was written by Ursula Ridley and published in 1971.

West Wittering 🐚

The Witterings (East and West) lie at the end of the Selsey peninsula. West Wittering has a very satisfying amount of folklore. Fig trees here, were, according to tradition, originally planted by St. Richard of Sussex. An Italian bird is supposed to fly across each year to sample the figs, visiting several places in Sussex including the village of West Wittering. Another legend is that King Ella, the Viking, lived in a local farmhouse. There was supposed to be an underground passage from this building to the church, possibly a smuggler's tunnel.

West Wittering had its own band of 'tipteers' (the Sussex name for Christmas mummers). The team consisted of six men, dressed in fantastic costumes, some carrying wooden swords. The script was handed on by word of mouth, but has been printed in the *Sussex Archaeological Society Collections*. The play opened with a preamble, by a character called simply 'first man'.

'Now your doors will open and we are come in,
I hope your favour we shall win;
Whether we rise or whether we fall,
We do our best endeavours to please you all.
Now the merry time of Christmas is drawn near,
We will show our sport in the pastime you have not

205

seen me (in) for one long year,
None of your ragged swords, but some of your loyal train,
We will cross the seas King George to please,
And home we will return again.
If you have not (a) mind to believe what I have got to say,
Send in old Father Christmas and he will boldly clear the way'.

The play proceeded in the time honoured manner, with Father Christmas, King George, Noble Captain, Turkey Knight (a variant of Turkish Knight) and the Doctor; the latter as usual offering comic relief. All completely predictable, until the final song with its trite 19th century chorus:

'We never miss a Mother till she's gone,
Her portrait all we have to gaze upon,
We can fancy see her there,
Sitting in her old arm chair,
We never miss a Mother till she's gone.'

This was evidently the final addition to the script, a daring attempt to bring it up to date, perhaps to satisfy the younger elements in the audience. Before any further changes or additions could be made, the play fell into disuse.

Wisborough Green

A huge green, providing the heart of an idyllic Sussex village. It won the best kept village competition for fourteen years, and one does not need to wonder why.

The almost circular pond was once used by the steam traction engines that pulled the caravans to the annual fairs. There was a pig fair, and later in the year a horse fair which meant a big turn-out of gypsies from all around the area. An old village saying is that no one can become a true resident of Wisborough Green without first falling in the pond.

206

There were several industries carried on in the village. In the Middle Ages the Hugenots brought their glass-making skills, and there were once limekilns, of which the Limeburners Inn is a reminder. Early in the 20th century as many as twenty boys were employed copse cutting. After they had completed the cutting, they would all sit in a clearing in the wood, with their axes stacked in the centre and banks of faggots around them.

The church of St. Peter and Vicula deserves an article to itself. The huge stone altar was hidden during the dark days of the Reformation, and used as a mantelpiece and a seat in the vicarage garden, before being reinstated in 1937. In the Middle Ages this was a place of pilgrimage, with many relics including it was said the cloak of St Thomas a Becket.

This was Canadian country during the Second World War, and the area teemed with troops and vehicles prior to D Day. When I visited Canada, I stayed at a motel, and the owner turned out to be an ex-Canadian soldier who had become a Sussex fan during the war, when he had been stationed in this very area.

Older people usually refer to the village merely as Green, as in the folk rhyme:

'Rudgick for Riches,
Green for poors....'

Woolbeding

The Domesday Survey mentioned 'A mill, 23 acres of meadow, a wood and a church.' Sounds like a nice place, as indeed it still is.

Woolbeding House has in its grounds a ten foot Italian fountain, believed to have come from Cowdray. Now owned by the National Trust, but not open to the public.

In the 18th century Charlotte Smith who wrote around forty novels and collections of poems, lived in the Rectory. Twentieth century readers either do not know her, or are not interested; but her contemporaries thought highly of her talents. Although she did not spend all her life in Sussex, she loved the county and its charms; as this extract from her *To the*

South Downs proclaims:

'Ah! hills belov'd – where once a happy child,
Your beechen shades, 'your turf, your flowers among',
I wove your bluebells into garlands wild,
And woke your echoes with my artless song,
Ah! hills belov'd – your turf, your flowers remain;
But can they peace to this sad breast restore;
For one poor moment soothe the sense of pain,
And teach a breaking heart to throb no more?'

Worth 🐾

Worth church has been called the finest in England. It is the largest to retain its Saxon foundations, cruciform in shape with an apsidal chancel. It dates from the 10th or early 11th century, and staid archaeologists have been known to become quite rapturous over its many treasures. On the north side is a 'Devil's door', which was said to be left open at baptisms so that the evil one could depart as quickly as possible. There are many stones in the churchyard of interest. For instance the unique headstone depicting a bell, in memory of Isaac Tullett, a bellringer who died in 1897. The inscription reads 'for upwards of fifty years a bell ringer at this church.' Another inscription is very concise: 'Here lyeth y body of James Coleman who died June 1746 by a fall from a wagon. Aged 68 years.' There are some graves with a curious, almost comical face on the reverse side. The conjecture is that they are stonemasons' trademarks, although they seem rather inappropriate.

Hundreds of years after the church was built, Worth found itself in the middle of England's great industrial area. Here the ironmasters of the wealden forests worked day and night and became the new rich. Later still the railway brought employment and new prosperity to the village, although not without some cost. In the parish records can be found such entries as '1904. Walter Fermore, late engine driver and Henry Tullett, late blacksmith, both of Three Bridges, the result of a railway accident.'

This is also literary country. Wilfred Scawen Blunt, poet and famed breeder of arab horses, lived at 'Crabbet'. About a mile away lived Frederick Locker-Lampson, the lyricist and collector. William Cobbett wrote his *Cottage Economy* at Worth Lodge, where he was inspired by Mrs Brazier, who had brought up forty children and grandchildren. It was said of her that she had done more work than any other woman in Sussex, and although she could not read or write, she could make bread, brew beer, keep cows, rear pigs and poultry, salt meat, produce honey and make candle-rushes.

To end on an even lighter note. This is Worth, commemorated for posterity in limerick form.

> 'An alderman living at Worth,
> Was famous because of his girth,
> He was rather annoyed,
> At his oblate spheroid,
> For he said 'it's the shape of the earth'.

Yapton

The saying is 'those who don't shut doors, come from Yapton'. (This is also said of people from other villages in Sussex, but Yapton seems to be the best known). There are several origins for the saying. One is that a Yapton farmer had a calf which got its neck stuck through a gate. To free it, the logical thing to do seemed to be to cut its head off. Ever afterwards, he decreed that his gates must always be left open. Another explanation is that in the days when windows were taxed, a certain gentleman in Yapton had as many of his windows as possible bricked-up. This made the house so dark that the servants had to leave the doors open to admit light. One lady told me that when her nephew (who actually lived at Yapton) left a door open at school, a teacher said 'You must come from Yapton'. He replied 'Yes, I do – but how did you know?' As a commentary to all this, the Yapton bell rhyme seems very appropriate:

> Shut the gate and clap'n,
> Says the bells of Yapton.'

Ghost stories seem scarce here. The only one I have been able to find is of a belief that the sound of polka music can sometimes be heard in the lanes leading in and out of Yapton, although the reason is not clear.

The wonderfully named pub The Shoulder of Mutton and Cucumber once appeared in the Guiness Book of Records, as the longest pub name in Britain. In 1898 in this inn, a Yapton thatcher named Marley was supposed to have sold his wife to a local ratcatcher for seven shillings and sixpence and a quart of beer. The pub yard was also the venue for the old game of quoits, which was played here, as in many other Sussex villages, in the 1930s.

In more modern times, Yapton May Day has seen the annual pram race round two and a half miles of the village streets. At The Lamb another modern game was played at the end of 1983. This was assegai throwing (actually a kind of arrow), and the idea was to throw them as far as possible – all for charity.

A rather more traditional game is that of conkers, and the horse-chestnut tree in Church Lane has been the local source of supply for many years. In 1980 the Parish Council found itself involved in an argument over who actually owned conker-rights in the tree.

Bibliography and References

Albery, William.   *A Millenium of Facts in the History of Horsham and Sussex. 947-1947. 1947.*

Allam, David.   *The Sussex Riviera: Aldwick Bay Estate. 1979.*

Anderson, Elizabeth S. (Ed)   *West Sussex as seen through the eyes of the W.I. 1975.*

Andrews, Colin.   *Shepherd of the Downs. 1979.*

Axon, William E.A.   *Bygone Sussex. 1879.*

Baker, Michael H.C.   *Sussex Villages. 1977.*

Barker, Susan and Hartley, Barbara.   *A Village Cookbook. n.d.*

Barty-King, Hugh.   *Sussex in 1839. 1974.*

Batten, John.   *West Sussex Villages. 1982.*

Beckett, Arthur.   *The Spirit of the Downs. 1909.*

Beckett, Arthur.   *The Wonderful Weald. 1911.*

Bentley, J.H.   *Copthorne People and Places. n.d.*

Bird, Ruth. (Ed)   *The Journal of Giles Moore. 1656-1679. 1971.*

Blaker, Nathaniel Paine.   *Sussex in Bygone Days. 1919.*

– *Broadbridge Heath Shelley School. 1983.*

Broadwood, Lucy E. and Maitland, J.A. Fuller.   *English County Songs. n.d.*

Brown, Lillian E.   *All about Bury. 1948.*

Budd, Mavis.   *Dust to dust. 1966.*

Budd, Mavis.   *Fit for a Duchess. 1970.*

Budd, Mavis.   *So Beautiful. 1981.*

Bull, D.J. and Oliver, L.K.   *Sussex Events and Disasters. 1979.*

Burstow, Henry.   *Reminiscences of Horsham. 1911.*

Charman, Aubrey.   *History of Southwater. 1977.*
Charman, Aubrey.   *The Memories and Local History of a Southwater Farmer. 1981.*
Cheal, Wilfred E.   *Amberley Heritage. n.d. Church of Holy Trinity, Poynings, Sussex. n.d.*
Clark, Paul.   *The Railways of Devil's Dyke. 1976.*
Cobbett, William.   *Rural Rides. 1830.*
Cook, C.F. (Ed)   *The Book of Sussex Verse. 1920.*
Cook, C.F. (Ed)   *Another Book of Sussex Verse. 1928.*
Cook, W. Victor.   *The Story of Sussex. 1920.*
Cooke, Arthur Stanley.   *Off the Beaten Track in Sussex. n.d.*
Cousins, W.L.   *Memories of Pulborough. 1980.*

Day, J. Wentworth.   *Here are Ghosts and Witches. 1954.*
Dudley, Howard.   *The History and Antiquities of Horsham. 1836.*

Eardley, F. Stenton.   *Horsted Keynes, Sussex. 1939.*
Edwards, Edward Tickner.   *Side-lights on Nature in Quill and Crayon. 2nd edition. 1912.*
Elphick, George P.   *Sussex Bells and Belfries. 1970.*
Errand, Jeremy.   *Secret Passages and Hiding Places. 1974.*

– *Ethnic. Volume 1 No. 2. 1959.*
– *Ethnic. Volume 1 No. 4. 1959.*

Fairless, Michael.   *The Road Mender. 1911.*
– *Folk Lore Record, the. Volume 1. 1878.*

Gibson-Hill, J. and
Henbery, E.W.

Ifield Mill. A Survey. 1979.

Glover, Judith.

The Place Names of Sussex. 1975.

Gordon, Rev. H.D.

A History of Harting. 1877.

Gray, Adrian.

The London to Brighton Line. 1841-1977. 1977.

Greenfield, John Osborne.

Tales of Old Petworth. 1976.

Griffith, Edward.

The Selsey Tramways. 3rd edition. 1974.

Hailsham, John.

Idlehurst. 1898.

Hall, Helena.

William Allen. 1770-1843. 1954.

Hall, Helena.

Lindfield, Past and Present. 1960.

Hamer, John.

By Wapple Way. 1980.

Handcross, C.P.

School Centenary. 1878-1978. 1978.

Hannah, Ian C.

The Sussex Coast. 1912.

Hanson, Ellen and
Warner, Renate.

Quakers in Ifield. 1976.

Harrison, David.

Hayward, R.L.

Yesterday in Sullington. 1969.

Hickman, M.M.

The History of Shipley. 1947.

Holmes, Edric.

Seaward Sussex. 1920.

Hopkins, G. Thurston and
Thurston, R.

Literary Originals of Sussex. 1936.

Hopkins, R. Thurston.

The Lure of Sussex. 1928.

Horsfield, Thomas Walker.

The History, Antiquities and Topography of the County of Sussex. 1835.

Hudson, W.H.

Nature in Downland. 1900.

Hurst, Lady.

History and Antiquities of Horsham. 1889.

– *Kelly's Directory of Sussex. 1903.*

Kendall, S.C. (Ed)

The Sussex County Book. 1938.

Kipling, Rudyard.   *Rewards and Fairies. 1910.*

Laker, T.J.   *Down Memory Lane. 1979.*
Laker, T.J.   *Yesterday's Child. 1981.*
Latham, Charlotte.   *Some West Sussex Superstitions lingering in 1868. 1878.*
Leigh, Lorma.   *The Roadmender Country.1922.*
– *Limeburning and the Amberley Chalk Pits. 1979.*
Lucas, E.V.   *Highways and Byways in Sussex. 1904.*

MacDermott, K.H.   *Sussex Church Music in the Past. 1922.*
MacDermott, K.H.   *Bosham Church: It's History and Antiquities. 1926.*
MacDermott, K.H.   *The Old Church Gallery Musicians. 1948.*
MacDermott, Richard and Richard.   *The Standing Windmills of East Sussex. 1978.*
MacDermott, Richard and Richard.   *The Standing Windmills of West Sussex. 1978.*
Martin, Edward A.   *Life in a Sussex Windmill. 1921.*
Marwood, Geoffrey W.   *The Stone Coffins of Bosham Church. 1974.*
Mee, Arthur.   *The King's England-Sussex. 1937.*
Migeod, F.W.H.   *Worthing: A Survey of Times Past and Present. 1938.*
Mitchell, Henry.   *On the early traditions of Bosham. (in Sussex Archaeological Collections. Volume XVIII. 1866).*
Mundy, Percy D.   *Memorials of Old Sussex. 1909.*

Nairn, Ian and
Pevsner, Nikolaus   *The Buildings of England-*
                                     Sussex. 1965.
– Nuthurst. 1977. 1977.

Paddon, J.B.   *Sequestered Vale of Sussex.*
                                       n.d.
Palmer, Roy. (Ed)   *Folk Songs Collected by Ralph*
                                       Vaughan Williams. 1983.
Palmer, William Scott and   *Michael Fairless. Life and*
Haggard, A.M.   *Writings. 1913.*
Parish, Rev. W.D.   *A Dictionary of Sussex*
                                       Dialect (Expanded by Helena
                                       Hall). 1957.
– Patching and its Church n.d.
Perham, M.R.   *Harting Old Club. 1958.*
Perthen, Barry.   *Rudgwick Celebrations. 1977.*
Phillips, W.W.A. and   *The Natural History of*
Kraunsoe, I.   *Pagham Harbour. Part 1. 1979.*

Ray, Roger.   *Around Old Handcross. 1980.*
Rayner, John.   *Eleven Songs. 1971.*
Rayner, R.W. (Ed).   *The Natural History of*
                                         Pagham Harbour. Part II.
                                         1981.
Rees, Arthur J.   *Old Sussex and her Diarists.*
                                         1929.
Rees, Josephine Duggan.   *Portrait of Slindon. 1969.*
Rickard, Rev. H.   *Amberley: Its Castle, Church*
                                         and History. 1923.
Ridley, Ursula.   *The Story of a Forest Village.*
                                         West Hoathly. 1971.
Rush, Philip.   *Great Men of Sussex. 1956.*

Saunders-Jacobs, Sylvia.   *West Chiltington in Sussex.*
                                         n.d.
Scott, G.   *All Saints Church. Roffey.*
                                         1978.

Scott, Hardiman. *Secret Sussex. 1949.*
Secretan, Rev. Douglas L. *Balcombe. 1937.*
Serraillier, Ian. *All Change at Singleton. 1979.*
Simpson, Jacqueline. *The Folklore of Sussex. 1973.*
Sisson, Rosemary. *The Parish Church of St. Mary, Lyminster. 1974.*
Smail, Henfrey. *The History of Woods Mill. n.d.*
Staines, Rev. E. Noel. *Dear Amberley. 1968.*
Steer, Francis W. *Guide to the Parish Church of St. Mary the Virgin, Walberton. 1976.*
– *The Story of the Forest. 1971.*
Strudwick, I.L. *Pulborough. A Pictorial History. 1983.*
Stubbs, Ken. *The Life and Songs of George Maynard. 1963.*
– *Sussex Yesterdays. No. 1 and 2. 1980.*

Taylor, James. *The Sussex Garland. 1851.*
Tims, Margaret. *Poets' England. 5. East and West Sussex. 1982.*
Tudor, Alice M. *Fernhurst: The story of a Sussex Village. 1969.*

Unwin, Mrs. Cobden. *The Hungry Forties, c. 1900.*

Walker, Peggy. *Rudgwick Memories. 1982.*
Williamson, Richard. *The Great Yew forest. 1978.*
Wills, Barclay. *Shepherds of Sussex. c. 1938.*
Wolsey, Viscountess. *The Countryman's Log Book. 1921.*
Wolsey, Viscountess. *Sussex in the Past. 1928.*
Wolsey, Viscountess. *Some Sussex Byways. 1930.*
Wolsey, Viscountess. *Myth and Memory. 1934.*
Woodman, T.C. *The South Downs, 1901.*
Wright, Maisie. *Cuckfield – an Old Sussex Town. 1971.*

Young, Rev. Arthur.   *General view of the Agriculture of the County of Sussex. 1913.*
Young, Gerard.   *Chronicle of a Country Cottage. 1942.*
Young, Gerard.   *Come into the Country. 1943.*
Young, Gerard.   *The Cottage in the Fields. 1945.*
Young, Gerard.   *Down Hoe Lane. 1950.*

English Dance and Song.
The Evening Argus.
Sussex Archaeological Collections.
Sussex County Magazine.
Sussex Life.
The West Sussex County Times.
The West Sussex Gazette.

Index